THE NEW YORK CITY CAB DRIVER'S JOKE BOOK

THE ONLY BOOK THAT TELLS YOU...

The NEW·YORK·CITY Cab Driver's JOKE BOOK

WRITTEN AND ILLUSTRATED BY JIM PIETSCH

WARNER BOOKS

A Time Warner Company

WARNER BOOKS EDITION

Copyright © 1986 by Jim Pietsch
All rights reserved.

Warner Books, Inc
1271 Avenue of the Americas
New York, N.Y 10020

Visit our Web site at
http://warnerbooks.com

A Time Warner Company

Printed in the United States of America

First Printing: March, 1986

20   19   18   17   16

To my family
    where I first learned that
laughter makes life worth
    living

Acknowledgments

I would like to thank, first of all, three people who were of immeasurable importance in the creation of this book: Christine Baier, Frank Baier, and my editor and good friend, Patti Breitman.

I would also like to express my deepest appreciation to the following people, without whose friendship and senses of humor this book definitely would not have been possible: Berk and Barbara Adams, Becky Bowden, Stan Drake, Don Lathrom, Carl Lindahl, Tom and Jane Pandelakis, William Pietsch, Patti Pietsch, Mike Postol, Joanne Regan, Kerry Regan, Steve Sauber, Barbara Schulz, Jane Scribner, Steve Singer, Leonard Starr, Mark Wise, Mark Worthy, and all the Dover Rovers down at the garage, especially Arnold Torres, Chris Cherney, George Longo, George Paris, Greg Highlen, Marcial Garlitos, Mike Bernardo, Bill Avery, Tommy O'Neill, and Danny Ruiz.

And last but by no means least, I want to thank all the people in New York City who passed through my cab and told me their jokes or laughed at mine.

Introduction

On an average night of driving a taxicab in New York City, between 5 P.M. and 5 A.M., I meet approximately fifty people. Fifty people I have never met before and most probably will never meet again. People from the most widely varying backgrounds and positions imaginable. And, fifty people who are possible sources for new jokes.

Before I started driving a cab, I didn't realize that it is a talent to be able to remember and tell jokes. I have loved hearing and repeating jokes for as long as I can remember, and it has always been a very natural activity for me. I assumed that it was for everyone else, but it's not so.

The most common response I get to the question "Have you heard any good jokes lately?" is "I can't remember jokes." Many people have told me they just don't have time to try to remember them. But, I don't *try* to remember jokes; for some reason they just get stuck in my brain and can roll around in there for years. And although I have discovered that this ability (some might call it an affliction) is somewhat rare, I am happy to live in a city where the sheer number of people guarantees that I will meet many others like myself. As the saying goes, "In New York, even if you're one in a million, there are still eight others here just like you."

And there *are* many jokesters around. I have exchanged jokes with people as diverse as grocery store clerks, international correspondents, prostitutes, stewardesses, lawyers, doctors, famous and struggling actors, musicians, writers, recording engineers, dancers, managers of famous recording acts, bartenders, waitresses, comedians, actors in soap operas, market researchers, cab drivers, tourists from all over the United States and the rest of the world, florists, elderly women, beautiful women, drunken fraternity brothers, college students, gay people, straight people, travel agents, self-confessed Jewish American Princesses, housewives, Air Force pilots, surfers, book editors, priests, ministers, people in advertising, furriers, movie producers, video producers, Emmy Award-winning composers, party goers, outwardly seeming serious folks, club owners, restaurant owners, and English royalty. And since New York is such a center of fashion, jewelry, textiles, garment manufacturing, publishing, film, television, music, theatre, art, importing, exporting, banking, brokerage, finance, and tourism I have the unusual opportunity to hear jokes from people from all over the country and all over the world. Sometimes the jokes are regional and require some explanation, but most often they deal with the universal human condition and produce the same result: the universal best medicine, laughter.

I never let anyone tell me a joke without returning a few myself, and this leads to a very enjoyable sharing experience. When involved in this lighthearted give-and-take, one's natural inclination is to tell one's best, most favorite jokes, or the most recent joke one has heard. So I am in the unique position of hearing the latest and greatest jokes from many people. Sometimes

I even hear variations of the same joke, which means that when I repeat the joke myself, I can use the funniest version. You might say that I have my thumb on the joke pulse of New York City. Maybe even the world.

Realizing that I am probably in the best of all possible situations to hear new jokes, I decided to put them all together and write *The New York City Cab Driver's Joke Book*. In presenting my collection I apologize to anyone who might be at all offended by any of these jokes. I decided, though, that in keeping with the "melting pot" spirit of this city, I would include all the jokes I heard, regardless of their subject matter, ethnic background or questionable taste. This is an accurate sampling of the jokes going around New York, and, although I may not agree with the viewpoints expressed by their humor, these are the jokes I heard, as I heard them. (Not everything in this book is a joke, however. *The parts in italics are real-life episodes*.)

I also apologize to any nonmusicians reading this book. Jokes dealing with the music business happen to be personal favorites of mine, so I have included a number of them here, even though they may not be completely understood by those outside "the business." You see, like many cab drivers who are writers, actors, and comedians, I am a musician and an artist, supporting my dream by driving a taxi.

No matter where I am, though, I have found that exchanging jokes is great fun for most people. As a matter of fact, often just the question "Have you heard any good jokes lately?" elicits laughter. And if the answer is "No," it's usually followed by "Have you?" Almost everyone likes to hear a good one, and I am only too happy to oblige. Hearing laughter from the back of my cab, and looking into the rearview mirror to see smiling faces, can make my evening quite enjoyable. This book, I hope, will bring some of this enjoyment to you.

An old Irish man is lying in bed, very ill. His son is sitting by the bedside, expecting the end to come at any moment. The old man looks up at the boy and says, "Son, I want you to go for the Protestant minister."

The son is totally taken aback. "But, Dad," he says, "you were raised a good Catholic! What in the world would ye be wanting with the minister at a time like this?"

The old man looks up and says, "Son, please. It's me last request. Get the minister for me!"

"But, Dad," cries the son, "you raised me a good Catholic. You've been a good Catholic all your life. It's the *priest* ye want now, not the minister!"

The old man manages to croak out the words, "Son, if you respect your father, you'll get the minister for me."

So the father prevails, and the son goes out and gets the minister. They come back to the house, and the minister goes into the old man's room and converts him. As the minister is leaving the house, he passes Father O'Malley coming in the door at quite a clip.

The minister stares solemnly into the eyes of the priest. "I'm afraid you're too late, Father," he says. "He's a Protestant now."

Father O'Malley runs up the steps and bursts into the old man's room. "Pat! Pat! Why did ye do it?" he cries. "You were raised a good Catholic! We went to St. Mary's together! You were there when I performed my first mass! Why in the world would ye do such a thing at a time like this?

"Well," the old man says as he looks up at his

friend, "I figured if somebody had to go, it was better one of *them* than one of *us*."

*   *   *

Q: Did you hear about the new Japanese–Jewish restaurant?

A: It's called So-Sumi.

*   *   *

A newlywed couple is getting undressed on their wedding night. The husband, after removing his trousers, tosses them over to his new bride. "Put those on," he says.

The wife looks at him curiously. "What did you say?"

"Go ahead, put them on," he says.

Well . . . okay," she replies, and she puts the trousers on. However, even after fastening the belt, they are still too large for her, and they just fall down around her ankles. "I can't wear these," she says.

The husband looks at her. "*All right,*" he says, "now just *remember* that. *I'm* the one who wears the pants in this family. And don't *you* forget it!"

So the wife slips off her panties and throws them to her husband.

"Put those on," she says.

"What? What are you talking about?" he asks.

3

"Go ahead," says the bride. "You made *me* do it, now you go ahead and put *those* on."

"Well, okay," he says, and starts to put the panties on. But they're much too small, and he can't even get them up past his thighs.

"I can't get into these," he says.

The bride looks at him and says, "That's right— and you're not *going* to, either, until you change your attitude!"

*   *   *

A guy and his girlfriend got into my cab, and I asked them if they'd heard any good jokes. The woman said, "Tell him the potato joke." The guy said, "You tell it." Then I heard them whispering, back and forth, and finally the guy said, "Okay, I'll tell it, because this is sort of a guy's joke."

A Polish guy is walking along the beach in France. There are many beautiful women lying in the sun, and he really wants to meet one. But try as he might, the women don't seem to be at all interested. Finally, as a last resort, he walks up to a French guy lying on the beach who is surrounded by adoring women.

"Excuse me," he says, taking the guy aside, "but I've been trying to meet one of these women for about an hour now, and I just can't seem to get *anywhere* with them. You're French. You know these women. What do they *want*?"

"Maybe I can help a leetle beet," says the Frenchman. "What you do ees you go to zee store. You buy a leetle bikini sweeming suit. You walk up and down zee beach. You meet girl very qweekly zees way."

"Wow! Thanks!" says the guy, and off he goes to the store. He buys a skimpy red bathing suit, puts it on, and goes back to the beach. He parades up and down the beach but still has no luck with the ladies.

So he goes back to the French guy. "I'm sorry to bother you again," he says, "but I went to the store, I *got* the swimsuit, and I *still* haven't been able to meet a girl."

"Okay," says the Frenchman, "I tell you what to do. You go to zee store. You buy potato. You put potato in sweeming suit and walk up and down zee beach. You will meet girl very, very queekly zees way."

"Thanks!" says the guy, and runs off to the store. He buys the potato, puts it in the swimsuit, and marches up and down the beach. Up and down, up and down he walks, but the women will hardly even look at him. After half an hour he can't take it anymore and goes back to the Frenchman.

"Look," he says. "I *got* the suit, I *put* the potato in it, and I walked up and down the beach—and still nothing! What more can I do?"

"Well," says the Frenchman, "maybe I can help you a leetle bit. Why don't you try moving zee potato to the *front* of the sweeming suit?"

* * *

Two Russian friends happen to meet in Red Square. One of them says, "By the way, did you hear that Romanov died?"

"No," says the other man, "I didn't even know he'd been arrested!"

* * *

A big, burly, six-foot man has a very tiny head, about the size of an orange. He goes into a bar and everyone in the place is staring at him as he asks the bartender for a drink.

The bartender gives the man the drink and, unable to resist, says to the man, "I'm sorry, but I really have to ask. You're such a big guy and you have such a small head. What happened?"

"Well," squeaks the man, "I was walking along the beach one day when I saw this lamp half buried in the sand. I picked it up, rubbed it, and this beautiful genie appeared.

"She said, 'You can have anything you want.'

"I said, 'Okay, let's screw.'

" 'But,' " she said, " 'genies don't screw.'

"So I said, 'All right, then how about a little head?' "

* * *

When I was younger, we used to tell jokes about a dumb guy, always called "The Moron." Later, in junior high school, the "Dumb Guy" jokes somehow became jokes about Italians. Then, for some reason I never understood, they became Polish jokes.

Years later, when I traveled abroad, I learned that the English have Irish jokes (and vice versa), the Swedes have Norwegian jokes (and vice versa), Brazilians have Portugese jokes, and so on. It's a worldwide phenomenon. And it's no wonder these jokes are so popular; they are often quite funny.

So—intending no slur—I have included quite a few jokes that just happen (as I heard them) to be about Polish people. Here is one:

6

The pope and the archbishop are talking, and the archbishop happens to mention that he heard a good joke the other day. The pope says, "Oh, I like jokes—let me hear it."

The archbishop says, "Okay, this is a good one! There were two Polacks walking down the street, and—"

Immediately the pope interrupts him. "Excuse me, but are you aware of the fact that *I* happen to be Polish?" he asks.

The archbishop is shocked. "Oh, my gosh," he says, "that's right! I'm . . . I'm really sorry. There . . . were . . . two . . . Polacks . . . walking . . . down . . . the . . . street . . . "

* * *

A man is driving across the country, and somewhere in the Midwest he stops off in a small town to have a quick beer. He parks in front of a little bar and goes in. There are about eight or nine locals sitting around drinking, and as the traveler sits at the bar sipping his beer, he hears a man call out, "Twenty-seven!" Everyone in the bar bursts into laughter.

Another guy calls out, "Nineteen!" And again everyone laughs. The first guy calls out, "Thirty-six!" And once again everyone laughs. Everyone, of course, except the traveler, who is totally baffled. So he leans over to the bartender and in a low voice asks, "Hey, what's going on here? Why are these guys calling out numbers, and why is everyone laughing?"

"Oh," says the bartender, "you see, this is a very small town. Everyone here knows each other so well that they all know each other's jokes. So they just assign them numbers, yell out the number, and everyone knows which joke it is.''

"Wow," says the stranger. "That's amazing!" So after a couple more beers, he turns to the room and calls out, "Nineteen!"

There is a dead silence. He calls out, "Twenty-seven!" Nothing. "Thirty-six!" He's met with more silence. So he turns to the bartender and says, "Hey, I heard those numbers called out before, and everybody laughed. What's wrong?"

"Well, you know," says the bartender, "some people can tell 'em and some can't."

*   *   *

A man is making love to a married woman when suddenly they hear her husband coming home. "Quick!" says the woman, "jump out the window!"

Before the man can even put on any clothes, he jumps out the window, totally naked. At that moment, the New York City Marathon happens to be passing by. So the man just falls into step and starts running along with the pack.

A man running next to him looks over and says, "Tell me something, do you always run naked?"

"Yep," says the man, as he keeps jogging along.

"Tell me something else," says the other man. "Do you always wear a condom when you run?"

"Only," says the man, "when it looks like rain."

*　　*　　*

Q: What do a moped and an extremely fat woman have in common?

A: They're both fun to ride until one of your friends see you with them.

* * *

A priest and a rabbi are out fishing one day when the priest says to the rabbi, "Abe, you and I have been good friends for quite some time now, right?"

"Yes," says the rabbi.

"Well, do you mind if I ask you a rather personal question?" inquires the priest.

"Why, no," his friend says. "Go right ahead."

"Tell me," says the priest, leaning in a littler closer and lowering his voice, "have you ever eaten pork?"

"Well," says the rabbi, "yes, I will admit that once I did have some pork."

"Tastes pretty good, doesn't it?" says the priest.

"Yeah, I must say that it did," replies the rabbi. He then says to the priest, "Do you mind if I ask *you* a personal question?"

"Why, no, of course not," answers the priest.

"Then tell me something," says the rabbi, looking around. "Have you ever slept with a woman?"

"Yes," says the priest. "I must admit that I have."

The rabbi leans closer to his friend and says, "Sure beats the taste of pork, doesn't it?"

* * *

Q: What would you get if Ella Fitzgerald married Darth Vader?

A: Ella Vader.

* * *

A policeman is walking down the street when he sees a man holding a young boy by the shoulders and shaking him violently. The cop quickly walks up to them and says, "Hey! What's going on here?"

"Well, you see, officer," the man says, continuing to shake the boy, "I'm a bass player. I was playing in that club right there when this little jerk ran in and twisted one of the tuning pegs on my bass!"

"I can see why you're angry," says the policeman, "but is that any reason to *brutalize* the kid?"

The man begins to shake the kid even harder and says, "Yeah, but the snotty little brat won't tell me *which one*!"

* * *

A doctor calls his patient to give him the results of his tests. "I have some bad news and some worse news," says the doctor. The *bad* news is that you only have 24 hours to live."

"Oh, no," says the patient. "What could possibly be worse than that?"

The doctor answers, "I've been trying to reach you since yesterday."

* * *

Q: Did you hear about the new lesbian sneakers?
A: They were called Dykies. However, they had to be recalled because the tongues weren't long enough.

* * *

11

A young woman is going to marry a Greek man. The night before the wedding, her mother takes her aside. "Now, look," the mother tells her daughter, "Greeks are a little strange. If he ever tells you to turn over, I want you to get out of bed, pack your clothes, and come home to me."

So the couple gets married and everything is fine for the first two years. Then, one night, while they're in bed, the man says to the woman, "Sweetheart, roll over now."

She gets very upset, gets out of bed, puts her clothes on and starts packing her suitcase. As she is ready to leave, the confused man says, "Darling, wait a minute! What's the matter?"

Holding back her tears, she says, "My mother told me that you Greek men are strange and that if you ever told me to roll over, I was to get my clothes on, leave you, and go home to her."

"But, honey," says the man, "don't you want children?"

* * *

Q: What do you call a cow with no legs?
A: Ground beef.

* * *

Two Polish guys go on a fishing trip. They rent all the equipment: the reels, the rods, the wading suits, the rowboat, the car, and even a cabin in the Maine woods. They spend a fortune. Then they drive eight hours to Maine.

The first day they go fishing, but they don't catch

anything. The same thing happens on the second day, and on the third day. It goes on like this until finally, on the last day of their vacation, one of the men catches a fish.

As they are driving home they are really depressed. One guys turns to the other and says, "Do you realize that this one lousy fish we caught cost us fifteen hundred dollars?"

The other man says, "Wow! It's a good thing we didn't catch any more!"

* * *

Q: Why won't a barracuda ever attack a Jewish–American Princess?
A: Professional courtesy.

* * *

Two New Yorkers are in Las Vegas gambling, and they win two hundred thousand dollars. One man says to the other, "Come on, let's go out and paint the town!"

"You know," says his friend, "I think this money is New York money. This dough is earmarked for the Big Apple, and I think we should go back there to spend it."

"You're right," says the first man. "Let's go out to the airport right now and catch the first plane back."

"Forget the airport," says the friend, "let's just take a limo."

"Forget the limo," says the first man, and then he yells, "Taxi!"

A cab pulls up in front of the two men. The friend

opens the door and is about to get in when the first man says to him, "Say, where in New York do you live?"

"Fifty-ninth Street," says the friend.

The first man then says, "In that case, I had better get in first because I'm getting out at Forty-third."

*   *   *

Q: What goes in hard and pink and comes out soft and mushy?
A: Bubble gum.

*   *   *

Dirty Ernie is sitting in the back of his first-grade class, a can of beer in one hand and a cigarette in the other. The teacher says, "Okay class, today we're going to play a game. I'm going to say a few words about something, and you try to tell me what I'm thinking about. Okay? Here we go.

"The first thing is a fruit, it's round, and it's red."

Little Billy raises his hand, and the teacher calls on him. Little Billy stands up and says, "An apple."

The teacher says, "No, it's a tomato. But I'm glad to see you're thinking.

"Now, the next one is yellow and it's a fruit."

Bobby raises his hand, and after the teacher calls on him, he stands and says, "It's a grapefruit."

The teacher says, "No, it's a lemon. But I'm glad to see you're thinking.

"Okay, the next one is round and it's a green vegetable."

15

Little Mary stands up and says, "It's a lettuce."

"No," says the teacher. "It's a pea. But I'm glad to see you're thinking." Then she says, "Okay, that's enough for today."

Just then, Ernie raises his hand and says, "Hey, Teach, mind if I ask you one?"

"No," she replies. "Go right ahead."

"Okay," says Ernie, "I got somethin' in my pocket. It's long and it's hard and it's got a pink tip."

"Ernie!" shouts the teacher, "that's disgusting."

"It's a pencil," says Ernie. "But I'm glad to see you're thinking."

*   *   *

Q: What do you call a boomerang that doesn't come back?
A: A stick.

*   *   *

A seventy-year-old Jewish man has worked in the garment center all his life and has never been married. One day a beautiful seventeen-year-old girl walks into his store to buy a fur, and it is love at first sight.

They get married and go to Florida for their honeymoon. When they get back, his friend says to him, "So, tell me, how was it?"

"Oh, it was beautiful," says the man. "The sun, the surf, we made love almost every night, we—"

His friend interrupts him. "A man your age! How did you make love almost every night?"

"Oh," says the man, "we almost made love Monday, we almost made love Tuesday..."

*　　*　　*

A man is playing golf and he hits his ball into the woods. He goes to retrieve it and comes upon a witch stirring a large cauldron of brew. The steam is billowing up, and the man stands there watching it, transfixed.

Finally he asks, "What's in there?"

"This is a magic brew," the witch cackles. "If you drink this, you will have the best golf game in the world! Nobody will be able to beat you!"

"Give it to me!" says the man. "I want to drink it!"

"Wait a minute!" she warns. "You will also have the worst sex life in the world."

The man pauses a moment to consider. "The worst sex life in the world? The best golf game in the world? Give me the brew."

The man drinks it down, goes back to his friends,

wins the game, and becomes the champion of the club. He goes on to play tournaments and becomes a big star. He is the best golfer in the country.

A year later he is playing at the same course, and he decides to go see if the witch is still there. He goes into the woods where he lost the ball the year before and finds her in the same place. He asks her, "Do you remember me?"

"Oh, yes, I remember you," she says. "Tell me something: How is your golf game?"

"You were absolutely right," he says, "I win all the time! I'm the best golfer in the country!"

She cackles and then says, "So how has your sex life been?"

"Not bad," he replies.

"Not bad?" she says, surprised. "Tell me, how many times did you have sex in the last year?"

"Three, maybe four," says the man.

"Three, four?" says the witch, "and you call that 'not bad'?"

"Well, no," he says, "not for a Catholic priest with a very small congregation."

* * *

Q: What do you call a man with syphilis, herpes, AIDS, and gonorrhea?
A: An incurable romantic.

* * *

A lady wants a few rooms painted in her house. She calls across the street to a man she sees doing some work over there, and he says he'll be right over. A few

19

minutes later the man leaves his crew, comes over, and the lady takes him into the living room.

She says to him, "I'll show you what needs to be done. First of all, this room should be painted white."

"All right," says the man. He goes over to the window, opens it up, and calls out, "Green side up!"

Next she takes him upstairs to her bedroom and says, "I think this room would look good in a nice shade of beige."

The man walks over to the window and calls out, "Green side up!"

Then the woman takes him into the bathroom and says, "I think light blue would be a good color in here."

Once again the man yells out the window, "Green side up!"

"Wait a minute," says the woman, "I don't understand. I thought for a minute that maybe you had a code here or something. But how come one room is white, one room is beige, and another one is blue, and they're all 'green side up'?"

"On, no, lady," says the man. "That has nothing to do with your rooms. It's just that I have a Polish guy across the street laying some sod."

* * *

Q: What do you get when you cross a computer with a prostitute?
A: A fucking know-it-all.

* * *

The pope and a lawyer happen to die at the same time and are standing together at the gates of heaven. St. Peter says to them, "Ah, gentlemen, we've been expecting you. Your rooms are ready." He turns to the lawyer and says, "Excuse me for a moment while I take the pope to his room. I will return presently and will then show you to your quarters."

"Gee," says the lawyer, "I wouldn't mind tagging along with you while you take the pope to his room. That is, of course, if you don't mind."

"We would be delighted," says St. Peter, looking at the pope. The pope smiles, and they all proceed through the pearly gates.

They arrive at the pope's room, and St. Peter opens the door. The room has a twin bed, a couple of chairs, a little table, a thirteen-inch color TV, and looks pretty much like a room in a Holiday Inn.

Taking his leave of the thankful pope, St. Peter then escorts the lawyer to his room. He opens the door, and the lawyer is shocked to see a palatial suite complete with balcony, king-size bed, spiral staircase, color TV console with remote control, stereo, VCR, plush carpeting, Jacuzzi, and a sauna. He is totally flabbergasted and says to St. Peter, "This room is terrific! But tell me, why is it that the pope, the leader of the entire Roman Catholic Church, got only a standard room, and I got this wonderful penthouse?"

"To tell you the truth," says St. Peter, "we have had many popes check in up here, but you're the first lawyer to make it."

*   *   *

Q: How can you tell when a lawyer is lying?
A: His lips are moving.

*   *   *

A man goes into the hospital for a routine circumcision. However, after he wakes up from the anesthesia, he sees a large group of doctors gathered around him.

"What happened?" he asks worriedly.

"Well," says one of the doctors, "we made a small mistake. There was a slight mix-up, and we performed the wrong operation on you. Instead of a circumcision we gave you a sex-change operation. We cut off your penis and gave you a vagina."

"What?" says the man. "That's terrible! You mean, I'll never again experience an erection?"

"Well, you *will*," says the doctor, "but it will be somebody else's."

*   *   *

A man down on his luck goes home to his wife and tells her, "Look, dear, we're low on money now, and we're going to have to cut down on some luxuries." He then adds scornfully. "If you would learn to cook, we could fire the chef."

"In that case," replies the woman, "if *you* would learn to make love, we could fire the chauffeur."

*   *   *

A drunk walks into a bar and sits down. In front of each stool he sees three darts. He calls the bartender over and says, "Hey! What are these darts here for?"

The bartender says, "Well, you take the darts and throw them at the dartboard behind the bar here, and anybody that gets three bull's-eyes in row wins a prize."

"Oh," says the drunk, stifling a burp, "all right." He picks up a dart and, weaving from side to side, hurls it, clutching the bar at the last moment just in time to prevent himself from falling off the stool. Amazingly the dart lands firmly in the center of the bull's-eye.

He picks up the second dart, and with one hand on the bar steadying himself as best he can, he throws it. With his follow-through he collapses onto the bar, his head hitting the wood with a resounding thump. Incredibly, though, the dart lodges itself right next to the other one. Another perfect bull's-eye.

The drunk then pushes himself up off the bar, picks up the third dart, and takes careful aim with two eyes that are looking in different directions. As he throws the last dart he falls backward off the stool and lands in a heap on the floor. But miraculously the dart lands once again in the bull's-eye.

As he stands up and wobbles over to the bar the drunk says loudly, "I want a prize! I want a prize!"

The bartender, astounded, says to him, "Okay, buddy. Okay. You'll get your prize. Just hang on a minute." As he turns around the bartender thinks to himself, "What am I going to *do*? Nobody has ever won before. What am I going to give this guy?"

Looking around the bar, he sees an old aquarium in the corner. He goes over, rolls up his sleeve, reaches into the water, and pulls out a nice, medium-size turtle. He goes back behind the bar and walks up to the drunk. "Okay, pal," he says, "here's your prize!"

The drunk's bloodshot eyes light up for an instant and he says, "Thanks a lot!" He then takes the turtle and staggers out of the bar.

A couple of weeks pass and then one day the same drunk stumbles back into the bar. He sits down at the same stool and calls out to the bartender, "I wanna try for a prize! I wanna try for a prize!"

The bartender walks over and says, "All right, buddy, go ahead."

The drunk then manages to repeat his previous performance with the one difference being that this time he manages to fall off the bar stool after every shot. However, he does make the three bull's-eyes.

"I want a prize!" he shouts. "I want a prize!" The bartender is totally flabbergasted. He says to the drunk, "I can't believe it! Nobody has ever done this before, and you've done it twice in a row!"

The drunk says, "Well, give me my—gulp!—p-p-prize."

The bartender says, "To tell you the truth, buddy, I just don't know what to give you. What did I give you last time?"

The drunk belches, smiles dreamily, and says, "Roast beef on a hard roll."

* * *

A metalworker receives an order from a chemical manufacturer for a number of very large cages. When the man delivers the cages to the factory, he is ordered to set them up in the laboratory. He asks the scientist what he will be keeping in the cages.

"Oh," says the scientist, "we're going to be using some lawyers for some dangerous experiments."

"But," asks the man, "don't you usually use *rats* for those experiments?"

"Yeah," says the scientist, "but you know, you get so *attached* to rats."

* * *

A teacher says to her third-grade class, "Children, I'm going to ask each of you what your father does for a living. "Bobby," she says, "you'll be first."

Bobby stand ups and says, "My father runs the bank."

"Thank you," says the teacher. "Sarah?"

Sarah stands up and tells the teacher, "My father is a chef."

"Thank you, Sarah," she says. "Joey?"

Joey stands up and announces, "My father plays piano in a whorehouse."

The teacher becomes very upset and changes the subject to arithmetic.

Later that day, after school, the teacher goes to Joey's house and knocks on the door. The father answers it and says, "Yes? Can I help you?"

"Your son Joey is in my third-grade class," says the teacher. "What is this I hear about you playing piano in a whorehouse for a living?"

"Oh," says the father, "you see, actually I'm an attorney, but you can't tell *that* to an eight-year-old kid."

*   *   *

Q: What do you have when you have one lawyer in a town?
A: Too little work.
Q: What do you have when you have two lawyers in a town?
A: Too much work.

*   *   *

Two friends, an Italian boy and a Jewish boy, come of age at the same time. The Italian boy's father presents him with a brand-new pistol. On the other side of town, at his Bar Mitzvah, the Jewish boy receives a beautiful gold watch.

The next day in school, the two boys are showing each other what they got. It turns out that each boy likes the other's present better, and so they trade.

That night, when the Italian boy is at home, his father sees him looking at the watch.

"Where did you getta thatta watch?" asks the man.

The boy explains that he and Sammy had traded. The father blows his top. "Whatta you? Stupidda boy? Whatsa matta you?

"Somma day, you maybe gonna getta married. Then maybe somma day you gonna comma home and finda you wife inna bed with another man. Whatta you gonna do then? Looka atta you watch and say, 'How longa you gonna be?' "

*   *   *

Q: How many actors does it take to change a light bulb?
A: One hundred. One to change the bulb and ninety-nine to say, "I could have done that."

*   *   *

A woman starts dating a doctor. Before too long she becomes pregnant and they don't know what to do. About nine months later, just about the time she is going to give birth, a priest goes into the hospital for a prostate gland infection. The doctor says to the woman, "I know what we'll do. After I've operated on the priest, I'll give the baby to him and tell him it was a miracle."

"Do you think it will work?" she asks the doctor.

27

"It's worth a try," he says.

So the doctor delivers the baby and then operates on the priest. After the operation he goes in to the priest and says, "Father, you're not going to believe this."

"What?" says the priest. "What happened?"

"You gave birth to a child."

"But that's impossible," says the priest.

"I just did the operation," insists the doctor. "It's a miracle! Here's your baby."

About fifteen years go by, and the priest realizes that he must tell his son the truth. One day he sits the boy down and says, "Son, I have something to tell you. I'm not your father."

The son says, "What do you mean, you're not my father?"

The priest replies, "I'm your mother. The archbishop is your father."

*　　*　　*

The phone rings in the home of a middle-aged Jewish woman. She picks it up and on the other end is an obscene phone caller. He begins telling her in great detail all the perverted, sexual things he wants to do to her.

Then she says, "All this you know from just me saying hello?"

*　　*　　*

A man goes to his doctor for a checkup and the doctor tells him, "I'm afraid I must operate immediately."

"But," says the man, "I feel fine!"

"I'm sorry," says the doctor, "but I just checked you and you *must* have this operation. It will be very difficult to perform, and it will cost you five thousand dollars."

"But I don't have that much money," says the man.

"That's all right," answers the doctor, "you don't have to pay it all at once. You can pay it in installments, paying a little every month."

"Oh," replies the man, "like you're buying a car."

"Yeah, I am," says the doctor.

* * *

One night in my taxi a woman and I were talking about jokes and humor in general when she said, "My mother told me that I am a clown, as opposed to a comedian. When I asked her what the difference was, my mother said, 'People laugh with a comedian. They laugh at a clown.' I said, 'Gee, thanks, Mom.'"

* * *

A well-dressed gentleman, wearing an overcoat and a hat arrives at a train station with two large suitcases. Because of their great weight, they cause him to walk in a very hunched-over way. He gets in line for the tickets, and just as a man gets in line behind him, he looks at his watch and says, "I think I'll start coffee at home. I should be home in about an hour." So, he punches it in on his watch and the computer starts his coffee at home.

Then he says, "I guess I'll check the stock market," and he pushes another little button on his watch.

Out comes the ticker tape, and as he reads it with interest, the man behind him in line taps him on the shoulder.

"Excuse me, sir," he says, "but I can't help but notice this watch you have. It's unbelievable! What else does it do?"

"Well, this button can tell the time in all different parts of the world; this button wakes me up in the morning; this button activates the calculator; this button interfaces with my computer at home. This watch can do just about anything." And in so saying, the man picks up his two heavy suitcases and, with great effort, moves a couple steps forward in line.

The man behind him is obviously impressed. "That's really quite remarkable," he says. "Do you think I could possibly get one of those?"

"Sure," says the man with the watch. "I could get you one, no problem." He thinks for a moment, then says, "Say, do you want this one?"

The other man says, "I couldn't take your only watch."

The first man says, "Oh, I can get another one. It's no big deal." He then slides his two heavy bags a few feet forward in line.

"Well," says the second man, "how much would you want for that watch?"

The man answers, "Why don't you give me three hundred dollars?"

"Three hundred dollars for this incredible machine? Wow! I'm glad I just went to the bank!" He takes out his wallet and says, "Gee, do you mind if I just try it for a minute right here?"

"No, go right ahead," says the man.

So the new owner of the watch puts it on and

pushes a button. The time in all different parts of the world comes up. He pushes another button and the ticker tape starts coming out. He pushes another button and up comes the computer readout. "This is just great," he exclaims. "Here. Here's the three hundred dollars. I've got to run and tell my friend."

And as he's running from the line the first gentleman calls after him, "Hey," he says, reaching toward the suitcases, "don't you want the *batteries*?"

* * *

Q: Where do you find the most fish?
A: Between the head and the tail.

* * *

A wife begins to get a little concerned because her husband has not arrived home on time from his regular Saturday afternoon golf game. As the hours pass she becomes more and more worried until at eight o'clock the husband finally pulls into the driveway.

"What happened?" says the wife. "You should have been home hours ago!"

"Harry had a heart attack at the third hole," replies the husband.

"Oh, that's terrible!" says the wife.

"I *know*," the husband answers. "All day long it was hit the ball, drag Harry, hit the ball, drag Harry . . ."

* * *

One night I was talking to a man, and after conversing for a few minutes, completely out of the blue he asked me, "If you woke up in the morning and found Vaseline on your asshole, would you tell anybody?"

I said, "No, I wouldn't."

So he said, "Well, would you go camping with me?"

*   *   *

A second-grade teacher says to her class, "Children, we are going to begin to study sex education. Tonight your first assignment will be to go home and find out what a penis is."

Little Freddie goes home and asks his father, "Daddy, what is a penis?"

The father pulls down his pants and points proudly, saying, "Son, *that* is a perfect penis."

The next day when the boy arrives at school, his best friend rushes up to him on the playground.

"Freddie! I forgot to find out what a penis is! What's a penis?"

Freddie says, "Come on."

So they both go into the boys' room, and Freddie pulls down his pants. He points down and says, "There: If that was a little smaller, it would be a *perfect* penis."

*   *   *

Two psychiatrists who are friends happen to run into each other on the street one day. One of them says to the other, "You're fine. How am I doing?"

*   *   *

A Polish man down on his luck sees a newspaper ad that reads:

WANTED: Male volunteer for Research Project. $500. Call for details.

The Polish man makes the call. They tell him to report the following morning and then give him the address. The next day he shows up right on time and is met by a man in a lab coat. He is taken into a room, and they explain to him what the research project is all about.

"The nature of this experiment," says the scientist, "is to learn what would happen if a male human mates with a female gorilla. Your job would be to have sex with the gorilla. Now, do you think you are still interested?"

The Polish man thinks for a couple of minutes, then says, "All right, I'll do it, but only under three conditions. Number one, I absolutely refuse to kiss the gorilla on the lips. Number two, I won't spend the night. After it is over I go home. Number three, the five hundred dollars will have to be paid in installments, because I just can't afford that much all at once."

* * *

33

An eighty-year-old woman is sitting on her porch one day when she sees an old lamp near the bottom of her steps. She picks it up, rubs it gently, and lo and behold, a genie appears. The genie tells the woman that he will grant her any three wishes her heart desires.

She says immediately, "I would like to be young and beautiful." And POOF! In a cloud of smoke she becomes a young, beautiful, voluptuous blond.

The genie says, "And what, madam, will be your second wish?"

The beautiful woman says, "I would like to be rich for the rest of my life." POOF! When the smoke clears, there are stacks and stacks of hundred-dollar bills all around her.

The genie then says, "Now, madam, what will be your final wish?"

"Well," says the woman, "I would like for you to

turn my old faithful cat, whom I have loved dearly for fifteen years, into a young, handsome prince.''

And with another puff of smoke the cat is changed into a tall handsome prince with dark hair and a glittering medal on his coat. The first thing the prince does is lean over to the woman and whisper into her ear, ''Now aren't you sorry you had me neutered?''

* * *

Q: What do you get when you cross a rooster and an owl?
A: A cock that stays up all night.

* * *

A man dies and goes to hell. He is walking along when one of the devil's associates down there tells him, ''It is now time for you to decide.''

''Decide what?'' says the man.

''You must now choose among these doors here the room in which you want to spend the rest of eternity.''

They walk along, and behind one door they hear screaming and yelling and glass being broken. The man doesn't even want to look in, so they just pass on to the next door. Here, accompanying the screaming and yelling, are loud explosions. The man quickly proceeds to the next door.

Behind this door is silence. The man says, ''Can we look in here?''

The associate opens the door, and the man sees a room full of people standing in manure up to their waists, drinking coffee.

"This doesn't look too bad," says the man. "I think I'll go in here."

He walks in, and as the door closes and bolts behind him, he hears a whistle and a loud voice that says, "Okay, coffee break's over. Back on your heads!"

* * *

Q: What's Irish and stays out all night?
A: Paddy O'Furniture.

* * *

Two Swedish guys get off a ship and head for the nearest bar. Each one orders two whiskeys and immediately downs them. They then order two more whiskeys apiece and once again quickly throw them back. They then order *another* two whiskeys apiece. One of them picks up one of his drinks, and, turning to the other man, says, "Skoal!"

The other man turns to the first man and says, "Hey, did you come here to bullshit, or did you come here to drink?"

* * *

Q: How can a bartender tell which men like Moose Head?
A: They're the ones with antler marks on their hips.

* * *

A man takes his wife and small son to the circus. At one point the father goes to the refreshment stand for some popcorn and soda.

36

The mother and son are watching the elephants, when suddenly the boy says excitedly, "Mommy, mommy, what's that thing hanging off the elephant?"

"That's his trunk," says the mother.

"No, no, no," says the boy, "farther back!"

"Oh," says the mother, "that's his tail."

"No, no" the son insists, "there! Underneath!"

"Oh! Ahem . . ." The mother gets all flustered and says, "Uh . . . uh . . . that's *nothing,* dear."

A little later the father comes back, and the mother leaves for a few minutes to go to the ladies' room. After she leaves the boy bounces up and down in his seat and says, "Daddy, daddy! What *is* that thing hanging off the elephant?"

"That," says the father, "is his trunk."

"No, farther back," says the boy.

The father answers, "Oh, that's his tail."

"No, no," says the son, exasperated. "What's that down *underneath*?"

"Oh!" says the man, "that's his penis."

"Oh," replies the boy. He then asks, "Well, how come when I asked mommy what it was, she said it was nothing?"

"Son," says the father. "I've *spoiled* that woman."

* * *

I often take taxies myself, and I know how frustrating it can be when you can't find an empty one. One time, after telling a particularly good joke to a woman, she said to me, "Great! Now I can tell that to myself in the morning when I am out there waiting for a cab."

* * *

A traveling salesman is driving through the country and stops at a farmhouse. He knocks on the door, and a little girl answers. The man looks down at her and says, "Hello, young lady, I am a feed salesman, and I would like to speak to your mother. Is she home?"

"Yes," says the girl, "but she's upstairs in the bedroom screwing the goat."

The man is quite surprised and asks, "But . . . but . . . doesn't that bother you?"

The little girl replies, "Naaaaah."

*   *   *

A man is on an airplane when the stewardess comes up to him and asks, "Would you like some TWA soda, some TWA coffee, or some TWA milk?"

The man looks at her and replies, "I want some TWA tea."

*   *   *

A Chinese man and a Jewish man are drinking at a bar. After a little while the Jewish man leans over and gives the Chinese man a strong punch in the arm.

The Chinese man is very startled and exclaims, "What's *that* for?"

"That was for Pearl Harbor," says the Jewish man.

"Pearl Harbor was the *Japanese*. I'm *Chinese*!" the Oriental man replies.

"Ah," says the Jewish man with a wave of his hand, "Japanese, Chinese, what's the difference?"

A little while later the Chinese man leans over and gives the Jewish man a hard punch on the arm.

"Hey, says the Jewish guy, "What was *that* for?"

"That was for the *Titanic,* the Chinese man says.

"The *Titanic*? asks the bewildered Jew. "That was an *iceberg*!"

"Ah," says the Chinese man, with a wave of his hand, "Iceberg, Goldberg, what's the difference?"

* * *

A woman says to a Martian, "Do you smoke after sex?"

The Martian thinks for a moment, then says, "I don't know. I never looked."

* * *

Louie is talking to his friend and says, "Guess what? *Everyone* in the world knows me."

"*Sure* they do," says the skeptical friend.

"But," Louie insists, "it's true!"

"Oh, yeah?" the friend answers. "Well, I bet Bob Hope doesn't know you."

"Okay, come on," says Louie. He takes his friend to the airport. They fly to California and go out to the golf course where Bob Hope is just teeing off. Bob Hope looks up and, seeing the two men approaching, runs up, shouting, "Louie! Louie! How have you been?" He gives Louie a big hug and insists on taking the two men to lunch.

After Louie and his friend have had lunch they leave the restaurant and the friend says, "Okay, Bob Hope knows you. But that doesn't mean *everybody* does. I'll bet your own senator doesn't know you."

"Come with me," says Louie.

The two men fly to Washington and go into the Capitol. As they enter the Senate Chamber Louie's senator stands up and says, "Gentlemen, Louie is here."

The senators all jump up and cheer, crowding around Louie. They adjourn for the day and take Louie and his friend to dinner. The friend is very impressed.

After dinner the friend says to Louie, "All right, I admit that probably everyone in this country knows you. But what about Europe? I bet Bjorn Borg doesn't know you."

The next day the two men fly to Sweden. At the airport they happen to run into Bjorn Borg, who is on his way to Monaco. "Louie!" says Bjorn, "I'm sorry, but I'm just leaving Sweden. Say, why don't you and your friend come to Monaco for a week as my personal guests?"

At the end of the next week, as Louie and his friend are sitting by the pool, the friend says, "Well, Louie, a lot of people certainly seem to know you. But you say *everybody* knows you, and I bet the pope doesn't know you."

The next day they fly to Rome. When they get to the Vatican, Louie walks up to the gate, and he is let in for a special audience with the pope. Louie tells his friend to wait in St. Peter's Square.

As the friend is standing in the square the pope comes out onto the balcony. The crowd lets out a roar. Then Louie follows the pope out onto the balcony and the crowd lets out another roar. As Louie and the pope are standing arm in arm waving to the crowd, Louie looks down and sees his friend faint.

Louie runs down into the crowd and gets to his friend just as the friend is coming to.

"What happened?" says Louie. "Was it too much for you that the pope knew me too?"

"That *was* very impressive," says the friend, rubbing his forehead. "But what really got to me was when a man came up to me, tapped me on the shoulder, and said, 'Hey, who's that guy with Louie?'"

* * *

A man is marooned on an island for ten years and has given up all hope of ever being saved, when suddenly, one day, a woman washes ashore. Her clothes are all tattered, and she is clutching a little waterproof bag. It seems that her ship also hit the coral reef off the island and has sunk. She, too, was the only survivor.

The man, overjoyed at seeing another person, blurts out his whole story, about how he managed to live on the island alone, how he learned to live off the land, surviving by his wits. When he has finished his story, the woman says to him, "You mean you've been on this island for *ten* years?"

"That's right," says the man.

"Tell me," she asks. "Did you smoke cigarettes before you were marooned?"

"Why, yes, I did," he says. "Why do you ask?"

The woman says to him, "Well, since you haven't had a cigarette in ten years, here!" And with that she pulls a cigarette out of her little bag and gives it to him.

"Oh, wow!" he says. "Thanks a lot!"

As she lights it for him she says, "Say, were you a drinking man before you got shipwrecked?"

"Well," says the man, puffing on the cigarette, "I *would* have an occasional whiskey now and then."

The woman reaches into her little bag and says, "You haven't had a drink in ten years? Here!" From her bag she produces a small flask and hands it to him.

He takes a pull from the flask and is thanking her when she suddenly says, "Gee, I just *realized.* You've been on this island for ten years. I guess you haven't, uh, *played around* in ten years either, have you?"

"Good God!" says the man. "Do you have a set of *golf clubs* in that bag?"

* * *

Q: What's the difference between a hobo and a homo?
A: A hobo doesn't have any friends at all, whereas a homo has friends up the ass.

* * *

A man goes in for a thorough physical examination. He comes in about a week later for the test results and says, "Well, what's the story, Doctor? Am I healthy?"

"Well," says the doctor, "I have some good news and some bad news."

The man says, "Give me the bad news first."

"All right," says the doctor, "you have a fatal disease and you only have about a week to live."

"Oh, no," says the man. "But tell me, Doc, what's the good news?"

The doctor asks him, "You know that great-looking nurse out there?"

The man says, "Yes."

"Well," says the doctor, "I finally screwed her."

* * *

Two Wasps are making love. Afterward the man says to the woman, "What's the matter? Didn't you like it?"

The woman says, "Of course I liked it. What gave you the idea that I didn't?"

"Well," says the man, "you moved."

* * *

One day the pope gets a phone call from God. God says to him, "Since you have been such a good pope, I wanted you to be the first to know."

"The first to know what?" says the pope.

God says, "I have some good news and some bad news. The *good* news is that I have decided that from now on, the world will have only one religion."

"That's wonderful!" says the pope. "Now everyone will be peaceful and get along with one another. That's great! But what's the bad news?"

"In a few days," says God, "you will be receiving a phone call from Salt Lake City."

* * *

Did you hear about the tight end who went to prison? He came out a wide receiver.

* * *

A mohel (the man who performs circumcisions in a Jewish ceremony) is retiring after forty-five years of service. Throughout his career, after each circumcision, he has put the little piece of foreskin in his wallet, taken it home, and saved it.

Over the years he has collected many huge bags full of these skins, and now that he is retiring, he decides that he would like to have something made from them. He goes to the best leather designer he can find and tells him, "I would like for you to take these skins and make something out of them that will represent my career and commemorate my long service to the synagogue."

So the designer says to him, "This is a very unusual request, but I will be happy to work on such a meaningful project as this. I will use all my skills as a designer and will make something for you that will be a symbol of all your years of dedication. I am rather busy right now, but I think I can have this done for you in about three weeks."

Three weeks later the mohel returns. The leather worker is very happy to see him and with a flourish presents him with a small box. As the mohel opens the box, he looks somewhat crestfallen.

"A wallet?" he says. "A small wallet is all I have to show for my many years of service?"

"But, my friend," says the man, "this is no ordinary wallet! If you rub it, it becomes a suitcase!"

* * *

A man got into my cab one evening. He was middle-aged and distinguished-looking in a friendly sort of way. When I asked him if he'd heard any good jokes, he told me this one:

A group of philosophy professors is traveling on a train in Scotland. They look out the window and see a black sheep grazing on the hillside. One of the men remarks, "Gee, I didn't know that the sheep in Scotland were black."

But another of the philosophers says, "Well, you can't really say *that*. You can only say that *one* sheep in Scotland is black. In fact, all you can say is that one *side* of one sheep in Scotland is black."

Yet another of the group adds, "Well, *really,* all you can say is that one side of one sheep in Scotland is black *some* of the time."

After hearing this joke, I said to myself, "This guy likes subtlety—a thinking man's jokester." So I returned with this joke:

Q: Do you know what the sadist said to the masochist?

A: Absolutely nothing.

He laughed and told me this one:

A medical student is taking a test, and one of the questions is, "Name the three best advantages of mother's milk."

The student immediately writes, "One: It has all the healthful nutrients needed to sustain a baby. Two: It is inside the mother's body and therefore protected from germs and infections."

But the student can't think of the third answer.

Finally, he writes, "Three: It comes in such nice containers."

I then countered with this:

The optimists says, "This is the best of all possible worlds. The pessimist says. "You're right."

The gentleman in the backseat beat me to the punchline on that one. He then told me this one:

This is a Russian fable: Once there was a man walking along a country road in the dead of winter. There was snow and ice all around, and the man, not having a warm enough coat, was shivering and hurrying to get home.

As he was walking, he happened to look down and see a little bird lying next to the road, all stiff and with its feet sticking straight up in the air. Feeling sorry for it, he bent over, picked it up, and put it inside his shirt next to his body, hoping that the warmth might help to bring it around. After about half an hour he felt a little flutter on his skin and was very happy that the bird was still living. But the man knew that what the bird really needed was warmth, something that he himself could not provide. Just then he happened to be walking by a cow pasture, and there, not too far from the road, was a steaming load that a cow had just dropped.

The man joyfully realized that this could provide the warmth that the bird so desperately needed. So he went over and stuck the little bird in the steaming pile. As he walked away he felt very happy with the thought that perhaps he had saved this little creature's life.

And sure enough, very soon the bird was revived

by the warmth. He was so happy to still be alive that he let out a loud, clear song of joy. Now a fox happened to be stalking nearby, heard the song, and followed it to the bird—and ate him.

Of course every Russian fable has a moral and this one has three: 1) it's not always your enemies who get you into it; 2) it's not always your friends who get you out; and 3) if you're in it up to your neck, don't open your mouth.

* * *

An elephant is walking through the jungle when she accidentally steps on a thorn. She is in great pain, but try as she might, she just can't get the thorn out. She tries to get it out with her foot, but you know how elephant feet are—they don't have fingers. She tries with her trunk, but even that doesn't work. She doesn't know what to do. Just then a little mouse walks by.

Desperately the elephant calls to him, "Little mouse! Little mouse! Can you please help me?"

The mouse walks over and asks, "What can I do?"

"I've stepped on this thorn," says the elephant, "and I just can't get it out. Can you help me? I would do *anything* for you in return—*anything*."

"Anything?" asks the mouse, his eyebrows raised.

"Anything," says the elephant.

So the little mouse goes over to the elephant's foot and, with both his hands and using all his might, he pulls and tugs at the thorn. Suddenly he yanks it loose.

The elephant sighs with great relief. "Thank you!" she says. "Oh, *thank* you! That's *so* much better—I can't thank you enough! Is there anything I can do for you?"

"Well," says the mouse, "you said *anything,* right?"

"Anything," replies the elephant.

"Well," says the little mouse, "I've been sort of checking you out in the jungle here for quite a while now, and actually, I sort of have the hots for you. So what I'd really like is to make it with you."

The elephant looks at the mouse incredulously. "*You,* a little mouse, want to make it with *me,* an elephant?"

The mouse nods. "That's right."

"Well," says the elephant, half smiling to herself, "help yourself!"

So the little mouse goes around to the back of the elephant and climbs up her back leg. He gets on top of her and starts going at it. Once he gets going he is really having a grand old time. He is just wailing away back there.

Meanwhile a monkey in a tree just above them happens to look down, sees what's going on, and thinks it's the funniest thing he's ever seen in his life. The monkey starts laughing hysterically, and he shakes so much that a coconut comes loose from the tree he's sitting in, falls down, and hits the elephant on the head with a wallop.

She throws her head back and cries in pain, "Ohhhh!"

The little mouse looks down at her and says, "Take it all, bitch!"

*   *   *

Did you hear about the new law firm of Dewey, Cheatham, and Howe?

* * *

A traveling salesman goes to a farm. As he drives up the road to the farmhouse he sees a pig with a wooden leg in the yard. When the salesman gets to the house and meets the farmer, he asks him, "Say, what's the story behind that pig with the wooden leg?"

"Funny you should mention it," says the farmer, "but that pig is the greatest pig I have ever had. One time I was doing the chores in the barn when I happened to doze off. Suddenly the barn caught fire.

"This pig," says the farmer, his eyes welling up with tears, "broke out of his pen, came into the burning barn, nudged me awake, and pulled me to safety. He saved my life!"

"Yes, I understand," says the salesman. "That's wonderful, but that still doesn't explain to me why the pig has a wooden leg."

"Well," says the farmer, "a special pig like *that* you don't eat all at once!"

* * *

Q: Did you hear about the man who had a penis transplant?
A: His hand rejected it.

* * *

An older man's wife dies, and a number of years later he decides that he would like to remarry. Shortly after that, he meets a woman he likes very much, so he proposes to her.

"Before I can give you my answer," says the woman, "I must tell you a few of my needs. First of all, I must have a condominium in Florida."

"No problem," says the man. "I already have a condominium there."

"Also," she says, "I must have my own bathroom."

"You've got it," he says.

The woman then looks the man in the eye. "And sex?" she asks.

"Infrequently," replies the man.

The woman thinks for a moment, then says, "Is that one word or two?"

* * *

Did you hear about the Polish man who locked his keys in the car? It took him nearly a week to get his family out.

* * *

Two men, both one year away from retirement, are working on an assembly line. One says to the other, "Last night I made love to my wife three times."

"Three times!" says his friend. "How did you do it?"

"It was easy," says the first man. "I made love to my wife, and then I rolled over and took a nap for ten minutes. I woke up, I made love to my wife again, then rolled over and took another nap for ten minutes. I woke up, I made love to my wife again, and then I went to sleep. I woke up feeling like a bull!"

His friend says, "Well, that *is* fantastic! I'm going to have to give that a try." So he goes home that night and goes to bed. He makes love to his wife, then rolls over and takes a nap for ten minutes. He wakes up, makes love to his wife again, then rolls over and takes another nap for ten minutes. He wakes up, makes love to his wife again for a third time, then rolls over, and falls asleep.

He wakes up in the morning and he's twenty minutes late for work. He throws on his clothes and runs down to the factory. When he gets to his station, the boss is standing there waiting for him. The man says, "Boss, I've been working for you twenty years, and I've never been late before. You've got to forgive me these twenty minutes this one time!"

The boss says, "What twenty minutes? Where were you Tuesday, where were you Wednesday . . . ?"

* * *

Q: Who had the first computers?
A: Adam and Eve. Eve had the Apple and Adam had the Wang.

* * *

Dirty Ernie is sitting in the back of his first-grade class with a beer in one hand and a cigarette in the other when the teacher says, "Okay, class, tonight I want you to find out what your father does for a living."

When the kids come back the next day, the teacher says, "All right, Susie, stand up and tell us what your father does for a living."

Susie gets up and says, "My daddy's a fireman."

The teacher says, "Good. Now, Billy, please tell us what your father does for a living."

So Billy stands up and says, "My dad is a policeman."

"Very good," says the teacher. So this goes on and on until it finally gets to Ernie.

When its Ernie's turn, he says, "My father eats light bulbs."

The teacher says, "What? Your father eats light bulbs?"

"Yeah," says Ernie defensively. "My father eats light bulbs."

"Ernie, what makes you think that?" asks the teacher.

"Well," says Ernie, "last night, before I went to sleep, I passed my parents' bedroom and I heard my father say, 'Hey, turn out the light and I'll eat it.' "

*   *   *

Q: What is the difference between a band that plays at weddings and a bull?

A: On a bull the horns are in front and the asshole is in the back.

*   *   *

A man working in a pickle factory has a tremendous urge to stick his penis into the pickle slicer. He is so overwhelmed by this desire that sometimes he is just barely able to contain it. He becomes very worried and goes to see a psychiatrist.

When he tells the doctor about his problem, the

54

psychiatrist says, "You know, I had a case similar to yours a few months ago. A man kept wanting to put his hand on a hot stove."

"What happened?" asks the man.

"The patient did put his hand on a hot stove," says the psychiatrist, "and he burned himself. But after that he never had the desire again. So my advice to you would be: If you have the urge to put your penis into the pickle slicer, follow your impulse and try it."

"All right," says the man, and he leaves.

When the man comes back for his next appointment, the doctor asks him if he followed his advice.

"Yes, I did," says the man. "I stuck my penis into the pickle slicer."

"And," asks the psychiatrist, "what happened?"

"Well," replies the man, "we both got fired."

* * *

A man is walking along when he sees a funeral procession going by. It is the longest funeral procession he has ever seen, with a long line of men walking behind the hearse. He notices that the first man in line has a Doberman Pinscher on a leash. After watching the long line of men for a few minutes, the man's curiosity gets the better of him, so he goes up to the first man in the procession.

"Excuse me, sir," he says to the mourner with the dog, "I'm very sorry to bother you in your time of grief, but never in my life have I seen such a large funeral procession. Could you please tell me who this funeral is for?"

"Yes," says the man, tightening the leash on his dog, "the funeral is for my mother-in-law. You see," he says, hanging his head, "my Doberman, here, attacked and killed her."

"Gee, I'm really sorry to hear that," says the other

man. "But...um...tell me, do you think maybe I could *borrow* this dog?"

The mourner points his thumb over his shoulder and says, "Get in line."

* * *

Q: Why are the lights brighter in the World Trade Center than in the Empire State Building?
A: The World Trade Center is closer to the Battery.

* * *

One night three convicts escape from a maximum security prison—a Frenchman, an Italian, and a Polish man. Running through the woods, they can hear the bloodhounds close on their trail. Fearful that capture is close at hand, the Frenchman says to the others, "Quick! Let's climb these trees!" Each man picks a tree and quickly scurries up.

Moments later, the police arrive at the first tree where the Frenchman is hiding quietly in fear. The dogs bark and paw at the tree trunk until the policeman calls up, "Hey! Anybody up there?"

Down from the tree comes the sound, "Whoo! Whoo!"

The policeman says to the other cops, "Come on, it's just an owl."

They proceed onward until they arrive at the next tree, where the Italian convict sits trembling in the leaves. Once again the dogs crowd around the trunk of the tree, barking and howling.

"Anybody up there?" shouts the policeman.

From the tree they hear, "Caw! Caw! Caw!"

"Aw, it's just a crow," says the cop. "Come on, let's go."

They hurry on until they get to the tree in which the Polish convict is hiding. The dogs stop and once again create a commotion at the bottom of the tree.

The cop shouts out, "Anybody up there?"

The gang of policemen hear a loud "Moooooo...."

* * *

Q: What did Adam say to Eve when he got his first erection?

A: "Stand back! I don't know how big this thing is going to get!"

* * *

A man is showing off his new rifle to his friend. He is especially proud of the fact that this rifle is equipped with the latest-model high-powered sight.

"Just look through that sight," he says to his friend. "You can see over three hundred yards! Go ahead! Look out the window and scan those rooftops way over there."

So his friend looks through the sight, and suddenly he lowers the rifle. "Oh, no," he says.

"What's the matter?" asks the man.

"I just saw," says the friend, swallowing hard, "my wife making love to a man on that roof over there." With that, he hands the gun back to the other man. "Here," he says, "I want you to shoot them for me."

"I can't do that," says the first man.

"Look," says the friend, "I don't know anything about guns. I can't shoot at all. Come on, you're my best friend, you've gotta do this for me."

"Well, all right," says the man. Having made that difficult decision, he begins to take aim.

The friend says, "Here's what I want you to do. I want you to kill them both! Shoot *him* in the balls, and *her* in the face!"

"Holy cow!" says the first man, peering through the sight and taking aim. "I think I can get this in one shot!"

*　　*　　*

I often get people in my cab who have just come from a movie or show, and many times I overhear their comments and personal reviews. On one occasion, however, a man and a woman were talking more about an audience member than about the dramatic Broadway show they had just seen.

"Wasn't that guy in front of us annoying," said the woman, "the way he was coughing and dropping coins on the floor every time he shifted in his seat? And always, of course, during the quiet moments of the show! You know, I counted seventeen coughs in the second act alone!"

"Yeah, I know," said the man, "and I counted a dollar eighty-five in change."

*　　*　　*

A man and a woman are about to make love, and the woman is getting very excited.

"Put your finger in," she whispers. So he does.

"Put another finger in," she says as her excitement heightens. So he does this, and she gets even more excited.

"Put your hand in," she says.

"My *hand*?"

"Yes," she says. "Your hand! Put it in!" So he puts his whole hand in, and she is going crazy.

"Put your other hand in!" She moans.

"My other hand?" He gulps.

"Yes! Yes! Do it!" she screams, barely able to contain herself. "Now," she cries, "clap!"

"I can't!" says the man.

She looks at him and says, "Tight, huh?"

* * *

Q: What do you get when you cross a computer and a Jewish-American princess?

A: A system that won't go down.

* * *

A teacher standing in front of her class asks, "Children, what part of the human anatomy expands twelve times when it is directly stimulated."

Little Susie, in the front row, starts giggling and laughing, trying to cover her mouth with her hand. In the back row, Johnny raises his hand.

The teacher says, "Yes, Johnny?"

Johnny stands up and says, "Teacher, the iris of the human eye expands twelve times when it is directly stimulated by light."

The teacher says, "Very good, Johnny. That's the correct answer. And, Susie, you have a very dirty little mind; and when you grow up, you're going to be *very* disappointed."

* * *

A tourist comes to New York. He goes up to a man on the street and says, "Excuse me, sir, but can you tell me what time it is, or should I just go fuck myself?"

* * *

Two old men are walking on the boardwalk. One of them says to the other, "I've got to run. I have to hurry home to make love with my wife."

The other man looks astounded. "Make love to your wife? You are as old as I am! Nearly ninety years old! What do you mean you have to go home and make love to your wife?"

The first man says, "We have a *great* sex life. We make love three times a day."

"You are kidding!" says the other man. "How do you do it?"

The man whispers to his friend, "Pumpernickel bread. That's my secret." And he runs off to meet his wife.

The other man starts to walk home. "Hmmm," he thinks to himself, "pumpernickel bread. Well, it's worth a try." So he goes to a nearby bakery.

He goes up to the woman at the counter and asks, "Do you have any pumpernickel bread?"

"Yes," she says.

"How much do you have?" asks the old man.

The woman replies, "We have a few *shelves* of it."

"Well," he says, "give me all the pumpernickel bread you have."

"All of it?" she exclaims. "It'll get hard!"

"How come," says the man, "*everybody* knows about this but *me*?"

* * *

A busy executive goes to the doctor for a complete physical.

The doctor explains, "We have a new computer that, with only a urine specimen, can tell us everything that is wrong with you."

"Great!" says the executive. "Let's do it."

The doctor gives the man a beaker. He goes into the men's room and comes out with a full container. The doctor then pours its contents into the computer. The computer begins to click and buzz and make strange sounds. After less than a minute it stops and issues a long computer printout.

The doctor picks it up and is studying it for a long time. Finally the man says, "What is it, Doc? Am I all right?"

"According to this," says the doctor, "you're fine except that you have tennis elbow."

"But that's impossible!" says the man. "I don't play tennis! I don't even play golf. I don't do anything like that!"

"Well," the doctor replies, "the machine is never wrong. At least it's never been wrong yet. But I'll tell you what I'll do. You take this sterilized jar home with you tonight. Urinate into it tomorrow, first thing in the morning, bring it in, and I'll run it through the computer once again, free of charge. How does that sound?"

"Fair enough," says the man.

As the executive is driving home he starts to think about the diagnosis and begins to get very angry about how computers are taking over the world. By the time he gets home, he has decided that he is going to "fix" that computer.

He gets out of his car and pisses a little into the jar. He then take the dipstick out of his engine and swishes it around in the urine.

Then he tells his wife and daughter about all of this and has them both urinate into the jar.

Finally, the next morning, before leaving home, he goes out behind a tree in his backyard and masturbates into the jar. He then drives into town, chuckling to himself.

"How are you this morning?" asks the doctor as he sees the man coming in.

"Fine, doc." He laughs.

"You seem to be in good spirits," says the doctor as he pours the specimen into the computer. Once again it begins to click and buzz, and in less than a minute, out comes a long piece of paper.

As the doctor studies it the executive says, "So, Doc, heh, heh. What does it say today?"

"Well," answers the doctor, "according to this, your car needs an oil change, your daughter is pregnant, your wife has gonorrhea, and your tennis elbow is going to get a lot worse if you don't stop jerking off like that."

* * *

A heavyset man got into my cab carrying a guitar case. He was going to a theater, so I asked him if he was playing in the show's orchestra, and he said he was. So we started talking, and I told him which shows I had played. We then started exchanging musician jokes. He told me this one:

In the old West a wagon train is crossing the plains. As night falls the wagon train forms a circle, and a campfire is lit in the middle. After everyone has gone to sleep two lone cavalry soldiers stand watch over the camp.

After a while they hear war drums start beating from a nearby Indian village they had passed earlier in the day. The drums get louder and louder.

Finally one soldier turns to the other and says, "I don't like the sound of those drums."

Suddenly, they hear a cry come from the Indian camp: "IT'S NOT OUR REGULAR DRUMMER."

I told the guitarist a couple more jokes, then he told me this one:

Two women are talking. One says to the other, "Say, you were going to go out with a French horn player. Did that ever happen?"

"Yeah," says the other woman, "it did."

"I remember you were really looking forward to it. How did it go?" asks the first woman.

"Well," says the other woman, "it went fine, and he's a really nice guy, but there's one major problem."

"Oh?" says the first woman, "what's that?"

"You see," says the second woman, "every time he kisses me, he wants to shove his fist up my ass."

*   *   *

A man once said to me, "My penis is four inches. Now *some* women like it, but some women *don't* like it that wide."

*   *   *

Two ninety-year-old Jewish men, Moe and Sam, have been friends all their lives. Well, it seems that Sam is dying, so Moe comes to visit him.

"Sam," says Moe. "You know how we have both loved baseball all our lives. Sam, you got to do me one favor. When you go, somehow you've got to tell me if there's baseball in heaven."

Sam looks up at Moe from his deathbed and says, "Moe, you've been my friend many years. This favor I'll do for you." And with that, Sam passes on.

It is midnight a couple nights later. Moe is sound asleep when a distant voice calls out to him.

"Moe . . ."

"Who is it?" He sits up suddenly. "Who is it?"

"Moe, it's Sam."

"Come on. You're not Sam. Sam died."

"I'm telling you," insists the voice. "It's Sam."

"Sam? Is that you? Where are you?"

"I'm in heaven," says Sam, "and I've got to tell you some good news and some bad news."

"Tell me the good news first," Moe says.

"The good news," Sam tells him, "is that there *is* baseball in heaven."

"Really?" says Moe. "That's wonderful. But what's the bad news?"

"The bad news," says the voice, "is that you're pitching Tuesday."

* * *

Q: Why did the Polish grandmother have her tubes tied.

A: She didn't want any more grandchildren.

* * *

Two men are business partners in the same office in New York, and they have a beautiful secretary. She's gorgeous, she's young, and both men are attracted to her. It turns out that they both start fooling around with her and she gets pregnant.

They don't know what to do, don't know who the father is, and they are in a real quandary. So they decide to chip in and send her off to Florida to have the baby. In her eighth month they send her away, but then they don't hear from her for quite a while, and they begin to worry.

One of the men decides to go down to Florida and

check on her. His first night there he calls his partner in New York.

"Well, how is she?" asks the man in New York.

"She's fine, she's okay," the man in Florida says, "but I have some good news and some bad news."

"Well," says the partner, "what's the good news?"

"The good news is that she is fine, she's healthy, and she had twins."

"Well, what's the bad news?" asks the man in New York.

The other man replies, "Mine died."

*   *   *

Q: Did you hear about the Jewish kid who asked his father for fifty dollars?

A: His father said, "Forty dollars! What do you need thirty dollars for?"

A man and a woman got into my cab one night. I had to look twice at the guy to make sure it wasn't Woody Allen. It wasn't, but he looked just like him. I told him that last joke. When we arrived at the destination, I turned off the meter and said, "Okay, that will be three-forty."

The guy said, "Two-forty! That's a lot! One-forty is an awful lot for a cab fare!"

*   *   *

A little boy walks into the living room where his parents are entertaining a large gathering of their friends and loudly announces, "Mommy, I have to poop!"

The mother takes the boy to the bathroom and says, "Now, Billy, the next time you have to go the bathroom, say, 'Mommy, I have to whisper.' "

"Okay," says the boy.

That night little Billy wakes up at three A.M. and goes into his parents' bedroom where they are sound asleep. He goes up to his mother and says, "Mommy, I have to whisper."

The mother drowsily replies, "I'm too tired now. Go whisper in Daddy's ear."

*   *   *

Q: How many doctors does it take to change a light bulb?
A: It depends on how much health insurance the light bulb has.

*   *   *

An Italian man sends his son away to the United States so that the boy can get a good education. Sending money from Italy, the man puts the child through junior high, high school, college, and eventually the son goes on to become a great success in business.

So the son decides to do something for his father in return. He makes up his mind that he wants to bring his father to the United States, and after some persuading, the father agrees to come.

The son flies him over and meets him at the airport. The son then takes the father home, and they have a big reunion party. The son sits the old man down and says, "Pop, what is it that you would like to do here in the United States, that you've never been able to do before?"

"Son," says the Italian man, "I woulda lika to see a baseballa game."

The son says, "Great! We'll go tomorrow!"

It just so happens that the next day is Old-Timer's Day at Yankee Stadium. The baseball greats are all there. The son has managed to get box seats right on the first base line. He gets his father a Yankees cap, a beer, and they are all set to enjoy the game.

The first batter up to the plate is Mickey Mantle. On the first pitch he swings that bat and CRACK! The ball goes flying.

The crowd goes crazy and the father stands up and yells, "Runna Mickey! Runna Mickey!"

So Mantle gets to second base, and the next batter up is Roger Maris. On the first pitch he hits the ball—CRACK! It goes sailing over the fence.

The crowd gets to its feet and the father jumps up and yells, "Runna Roger! Runna Roger! Run!"

The next batter up is Joe DiMaggio. The pitcher throws the ball.

"Ball one!"

"Ball two!"

"Ball three!"

"Ball four!"

Joe DiMaggio tosses his bat aside and begins to walk to first base.

The father yells out, "Runna Joe! Runna Joe! Run!"

The son says, "No, no, Pop. He got four balls. He walks."

And the old man clenches his fist and says solemnly, "Walka proud, Joe. Walka proud."

*　　*　　*

A psychiatrist decides he wants to test dogs to see if they pick up any characteristics from their owners. So he gets an architect's dog, a mathematician's dog, and a musician's dog.

First he puts the architect's dog in a room with a big pile of bones. Through a one-way window the psychiatrist carefully observes the dog's reaction. Right away the architect's dog builds a little skyscraper out of bones, then builds a couple of little houses and a little bridge. The doctor scribbles furiously, trying to write all this down.

Next he puts the mathematician's dog in the room with the pile of bones. Well, right away the mathematician's dog divides the pile into two equal halves, then divides those piles into two equal halves. The dog then takes two bones from one pile and adds them to the next pile, then takes two bones from that pile and adds them to the next one, and so on. The psychiatrist is writing like mad, unable to believe his eyes.

When the doctor is ready for the next dog, however, the musician's dog is a half hour late, eats all the bones, screws the other two dogs, then takes the rest of the day off.

*   *   *

Q: What crime did they finally get old King Midas on?
A: Gild by association.

*   *   *

A young boy is told by his very puritanical father that he should never have sex with a woman, because a woman has teeth in her vagina and might bite off his penis.

The years go by, the boy grows up, and one day he decides to get married. On his wedding night, though, he locks himself in the bathroom and refuses to come out. His wife asks him through the locked door what could possibly be wrong. The man calls out, "You have *teeth* down there!"

The woman says, "No, I don't. Come on out and you can look for yourself!"

So the man opens the door and the wife shows him. "You see! There are no teeth there."

"Well," says the man, "with gums like *that*, I can see why not!"

*   *   *

Q: How can you tell if a Polish man is at a cockfight?
A: He's the one with the duck.

* * *

Q: How can you tell if an Italian is at a cockfight?
A: He's the one betting on the duck.

* * *

Q: How can you tell if the Mafia is at a cockfight?
A: The duck wins.

* * *

A couple gets married, and the girl's mother lives downstairs. The girl has never made love to a man before, and on their wedding night, when he takes off his shirt, she goes running downstairs.

"Momma, Momma," she cries. "I can't believe it! He has hair all over his chest! I can't make love to him, it's disgusting!"

The mother says to her, "He's your husband, you do what he wants you to. Now go back upstairs."

When the girl gets back upstairs, the man takes off his pants. This sends her running back down to her mother, "Momma, Momma! It's terrible! He has hair all over his legs!"

The mother tells the girl, "Look, he is your husband, you are his wife. You go back upstairs and do what he wants."

The girl goes back upstairs, and the man takes off his shoes and socks. She looks down and sees that he of one of his feet is missing. She goes crying back down the stairs.

"Momma, Momma! He's got a foot and a half!"

"You stay here," says the mother. "*I'll* go upstairs."

*　　*　　*

A man walks into the doctor's office and the doctor says to him, "I've got some good news and some bad news."

"Tell me the good news first," the patient says.

"The good news is that your penis is going to be two inches longer and an inch wider," the doctor replies.

"That's great!" says the patient. "What's the bad news?"

The doctor says, "Malignant."

*　　*　　*

Some Polish people decide to start a chicken farm. They get some chickens and plant them in the ground, headfirst. When they all die, they are somewhat confused, but they don't give up.

They get some more chickens, but these they plant feet-first. It takes a little longer, but eventually the second batch of chickens dies also.

They decide to write a letter to the Polish agricultural bureau. In their letter they explain in detail the procedures they have followed and their disappointing results. A few weeks later they receive a reply from the bureau: "Before we can advise you, we need you to send us a soil sample."

*　　*　　*

Q: What's the difference between a snowman and a snowwoman?

A: Snowballs.

*   *   *

There is a new commander of a base of the French Foreign Legion, and the captain is showing him around all the buildings. After he has made the rounds the commander looks at the captain and says, "Wait a minute. You haven't shown me that small blue building over there. What's that used for?"

The captain says, "Well, sir, you see that there are no women around. Whenever the men feel the need of a woman, they go there and use the camel—"

"Enough!" says the commander in disgust.

Well, two weeks later, the commander himself starts to feel in need of a woman. He goes to the captain and says. "Tell me something, Captain." Lowering his voice and glancing furtively around, he asks, "Is the camel free anytime soon?"

The captain says, "Well, let me see." He opens up his book. "Why, yes, sir, the camel is free tomorrow afternoon at two o'clock."

The commander says, "Put me down."

So the next day at two o'clock the commander goes to the little blue building and opens the door. There inside he finds the cutest camel he's ever seen. Right next to the camel is a little step stool, so he closes the door behind him and puts the step stool directly behind the camel. He stands on the stool, drops his trousers, and begins to have sex with the camel.

A minute later the captain walks in.

"Ahem, begging your pardon, sir," says the captain, "but wouldn't it be wiser to ride the camel into town and find a woman like all the other men?"

* * *

Q: Why did the Polish man return his necktie?
A: It was too tight.

A man is skydiving, enjoying his free-fall, when he realizes that he has reached the altitude where he must open his parachute. So he pulls on the rip cord, but nothing happens.

"No problem," he says to himself, "I still have my emergency chute."

So he pulls the rip cord on his emergency parachute, and once again, nothing happens. Now the man begins to panic.

"What am I going to do?" he thinks. "I'm a goner."

Just then he sees a man flying up from the earth toward him. He can't figure out where this man is coming from or what he's doing, but he says to himself, "Maybe he can help me. If he can't, then I'm done for."

When the man gets close enough to him, the sky

diver cups his hands and shouts down, *"Hey, do you know anything about parachutes?"*

The man coming up cups his hands and calls back, *"No! Do you know anything about gas stoves?"*

* * *

A nun dies and goes to heaven. St. Peter says to her, "I'm sure you've lead a virtuous life, Sister, but before I can let you into heaven, you must answer one question. What," asks St. Peter, "were Eve's first words to Adam?"

"Boy," says the nun, "that's a hard one."

"That's right!" says St. Peter, and the pearly gates open wide.

* * *

It is World War II and a group of new recruits is going through basic training. Unfortunately, when the rifles are handed out, the supply runs out, and so one of the soldiers doesn't get a rifle.

The sergeant gives the man a broomstick instead and tells him, "When you need to shoot, just point this and say, 'Bangity, bangity, bang!'"

The man feels a little uneasy about it and becomes even more disconcerted when they hand out bayonets and he doesn't get one of those, either. Once again the sergeant takes him aside.

"If you get into hand-to-hand combat," says the sergeant, tying a carrot on to the end of the broomstick, "just poke the enemy with this and say 'Stabbity, stabbity, stab!'"

The soldier feels quite nervous about all this. But he figures the sergeant knows what he is doing.

So the company is shipped overseas and starts to see some action. During their first battle the soldier with the broomstick sees a few German soldiers running toward his position. He points the broomstick at them and says, "Bangity, bangity, bang!" He is amazed when they all fall down.

"Wow!" he says to himself, "it really works!"

Suddenly a German soldier jumps out from behind a nearby tree. Immediately the American pokes him with the carrot and says, "Stabbity, stabbity, stab!"

The German soldier falls dead at his feet.

"This is great!" the American says to himself.

Just then, another German starts approaching, so he points his broomstick and says, "Bangity, bangity, bang!" But the German just keeps on coming. After trying to "shoot" him a few more times the German keeps getting closer and closer, so the American says, "Stabbity, stabbity, stab!" But the German just keeps on coming.

Finally the German knocks the American down and walks over him. As the American is lying on his back being trampled, he hears the German saying, "Tankity, tankity, tank!"

*   *   *

Q: What's the difference between a prostitute and a rooster?

A: A rooster says, "Cock a doodle do" and a prostitute says, "Any cock'll do."

*   *   *

I have often wondered where jokes come from and have had many discussions about this with my passengers. One theory I heard was that jokes are made up in prisons.

The theory that I have heard most often, though, is that stockbrokers create many of the jokes. It is true that as soon as news hits the street, jokes about it mysteriously appear, and they do seem to emanate from the Wall Street area.

One night I was discussing this question with a fare when he told me that he had indeed met one of these brokers many years ago. The broker told the man that he had created many jokes and could, in fact, make up a joke about anything at all. He challenged the man to come up with a subject and the man said, "Okay, cowboys and Indians."

The broker thought for only a moment, the man in my cab told me, then told him a joke that went on to become very popular. This man then told me the joke, and I actually had heard it many years ago. You probably did too. It goes like this:

Two cowboys come upon an Indian lying on his stomach with his ear to the ground. One of the cowboys stops and says to the other, "You see that Indian?"

"Yeah," says the other cowboy.

"Look," says the first one, "he's listening to the ground. He can hear things for miles in any direction."

Just then the Indian looks up.

"Covered wagon," he says, "about two miles away. Have two horses, one brown, one white. Man, woman, child, household effects in wagon."

"Incredible!" says the cowboy to his friend. "This Indian knows how far away they are, how many horses, what color they are, who is in the wagon, and what is in the wagon. Amazing!"

The Indian looks up and says, "Ran over me about a half hour ago."

So now we know the origin of that old classic.

* * *

A man and woman are standing at a cocktail party when the woman says to the man, "You know, you look *just* like my third husband."

"Oh, really?" says the man. "How many times have you been married?"

The woman answers, "Twice."

* * *

One night in Washington, when Nixon was president, there was a heavy snowfall. When the president woke up in the morning, he looked out the window and saw a beautiful blanket of snow covering the White House lawn.

He was snapped out of his peaceful reverie when he noticed, written on the lawn in yellow snow, "Dick Nixon is an asshole."

The president got very angry and summoned the FBI and the CIA.

"I want that urine analyzed," he ordered them. "And I want to find out who the culprit is right now, *without delay*! This is *top priority*!"

Early in the afternoon a representative of the two agencies reported back in to Nixon. "Sir," he said, "we have tested the urine and we know whose it is.

However, there is some good news and some bad news. Which would you like first?''

"Oh, no," said Nixon. "I guess you had better give me the good news first."

"Well, sir," said the man, "we analyzed the urine, and it is Henry Kissinger's."

"Oh, no," cried Nixon, and then suddenly the realization hit him: "That's the *good* news? What could the *bad* news possibly be?"

The man answered him, "It was in Pat's handwriting."

*   *   *

A man is crawling along in the desert when he suddenly sees another man approaching on a camel. When the rider gets close enough, the crawling man says, "Please, can you help me? I need some water."

"I'm sorry," says the man on the camel, "I don't have any water. But I can sell you some neckties."

"Ties?" says the man. "I need *water*."

"I'll sell you one for four dollars."

"I need *water*," says the man.

"All right, two for seven dollars," says the man on the camel.

"Please!" says the man, "can you tell me where the water is?"

"Okay, okay," says the other man, "you crawl down about three more miles straight ahead. Just the way you're going. After about three miles you're going to get to a stone. When you get there, you're going to turn left. Crawl another three miles and you'll get to the

83

oasis. Are you sure you don't want a tie, though? Three for ten bucks? That's the *best* I can do."

But the man just gets slowly up onto his feet and starts staggering toward the water.

The man walks and walks and walks. Then he begins crawling again until finally he gets to the stone. He brushes the sand off it, and he sees an arrow pointing to the left. So, turning left, he crawls on and on until he sees some palm trees. He gets up on his feet and starts stumbling toward the oasis.

There is a man standing at the oasis, and the thirsty man asks him, "Is this the oasis? Can I get water here?"

"Oh, sure, there's plenty of water here," says the other man.

"Oh, great," says the man as he starts to stagger toward the water hole.

"I'm sorry," says the other man, "ties required."

* * *

Q: If athletes get athlete's foot, what do astronauts get?
A: Missile toe.

* * *

Statues of a beautiful naked woman and a handsome naked man stand facing each other in a park. One day an angel comes down and tells them, "Since you have both been standing here patiently looking at each other for twenty years without ever being able to do anything, I am now going to give you fifteen minutes to be real human beings to do whatever you want."

Suddenly the two statues become flesh and blood. Immediately, they run off behind some bushes. The angel sees the bushes shaking and hears the loud rustling of leaves, and lots of giggling. After ten minutes the man and woman come out from behind the bushes.

"Your time isn't up yet," the angel says. "You still have five minutes more."

"Oh great," they cry, and as they run back behind the bushes, the angel hears the woman say to the man, "Okay, this time *you* hold the pigeons and *I'll* shit on their heads!"

* * *

Q: Why was the Jewish-American Princess snorting Nutri-Sweet?
A: She thought it was diet coke.

* * *

Three women always hang their laundry out in the backyard. When it rains, however, the laundry always gets wet. All the laundry, that is, except for Sophie's. The other two women wonder why Sophie never has her laundry out on the days that it rains.

So one day they are all out in the backyard putting their clothes on the line when one of the women says to Sophie, "Say, how come when it rains, your laundry is never out?"

"Well," says Sophie, "when I wake up in the morning, I look over at Saul. If his penis is hanging over his *right* leg, I know it's going to be a great day, and I can hang out the wash. If his penis is hanging over his *left* leg, I know it's going to rain, so I don't hang out the wash."

"What if he has an erection?" asks one of the women.

"Honey," says Sophie, "on a day like *that*, you don't do the *laundry*."

*　　*　　*

A man is sightseeing in the mountains and is marveling at the wondrous beauty of nature. At one point he gets so absorbed in the beautiful view that he forgets what he is doing and walks off a cliff. As he is falling he sees a branch sticking out from the wall of the cliff. He reaches out and manages to grab the branch.

As he hangs there he begins to pray, "Oh Lord, please help me. I'm losing my strength and I can't hold on much longer. Please, God, please save me."

Suddenly the heavens part, and a voice comes booming down, "*I am the Lord!*"

"Oh, Lord!" cries the man, "please save me!"

"I will save you," booms the voice. "All you have to do is prove your faith in me by letting go of the branch."

The man looks down at the two-hundred-foot drop below him, thinks for a moment, then says, "Is there anybody else up there?"

* * *

A wealthy, ninety-five-year-old multimillionaire is meeting with his financial advisor. The advisor is very excited and tells the old man, "I just found out about an investment I can make for you which will *double* your money in just five years!"

"Five years? Are you kidding?" exclaims the old man. "At *my* age, I don't even buy green bananas."

* * *

A man is sitting at home with his wife. He says to her, "You know, I was thinking of going down to the bar tonight and entering that big-dick contest."

"Oh, honey," she exclaims, "I don't want you taking that out in public!"

"But, sweet thing," he says, "the prize is a hundred dollars!"

"I don't care," she says. "I don't want you showing that thing to everybody."

So he lets the subject drop until the following night when his wife walks in on him in the bedroom, counting out a hundred dollars.

"Did you go down and enter that big-dick contest last night after I told you not to?" she asks.

"Please forgive me, turtle dove," he says.

"You mean, you took that thing out for everybody to see?" she says, tears welling up in her eyes.

The man looks at her fondly and says, "Only enough to win."

* * *

Imagine my surprise when a woman told me these two!

Q: What do you get when you cross a rooster and M&M's?
A: A cock that melts in your mouth, not in your hands.

Q: What can a Lifesaver do that a man can't do?
A: Come in five flavors.

* * *

A Jew, a Greek, and an Italian man all die in a plane crash. They are standing before the Lord, and the Lord tells them, "I am going to give you all one more chance. I am going to send you back to the earth on one condition: that you give up your bad habits."

They all say, "We will, we will. Please let us live again!" The Italian agrees to give up eating compulsively. The Jewish man promises not to think of money all the time. And the Greek man vows not to constantly think about sex.

Suddenly they find themselves back on earth, walking down a street. Before they even get a chance to say anything to each other about what has just happened, the Italian man sees a restaurant and begins to salivate. He starts running toward the restaurant when POOF! He disappears in a cloud of smoke.

Just then the Jewish man sees a dime on the street a couple feet away. He steps forward, bends over to pick it up, and POOF! Both he and the Greek disappear

*   *   *

This joke was circulating during a particularly dismal summer for the Yankees:

Q: What do Michael Jackson and the New York Yankees have in common?
A: They both wear one glove for no apparent reason.

* * *

Washington is suddenly infested with rats. No one can explain why it has happened, but it has quickly become a serious problem. The government officials try everything, but nothing seems to get rid of the rodents. In desperation the government officials place an add for anyone knowing of any means to rid the city of this terrible nuisance.

One day a little man in a green suit shows up at the gate of the White House and asks to see the president. He is about to be turned away when he says that he has come in response to the advertisement. He is taken immediately to see Mr. Reagan.

"I can get rid of your rat problem in a number of hours," says the little man in a strange, unfamiliar foreign accent. "It will only cost you five hundred dollars."

"All right," says the president, "that sounds reasonable. You've got the job."

The little man then reaches into a sack he is carrying over his shoulder and pulls out a little bright green rat. He puts the rat down on the floor and walks out the door.

The rat follows him, and as the man walks through the city, all the rats fall in behind. They come from everywhere, and soon there is a huge horde of rats swarming through the city behind the little man in the green suit and his little green rat.

The man walks down to the Potomac, and the little green rat jumps in. All the other rats follow and are instantly drowned in the river, ridding Washington of its rodent problem.

President Reagan happily goes up to the little man and hands him five hundred dollars.

But the man refuses to take the money. "No, no," he says, "I have decided that this will just be a favor I have done for the president of the United States. Good day." And with that he starts to turn and walk away.

"Uh, just a moment, little fellow," says the president.

"Yes?" replies the man.

Reagan sidles up to the man and says to him in a low voice, "Do you, by any chance, have any little green Democrats?"

* * *

Q: How do you break a Polish guy's finger?
A: Punch him in the nose.

* * *

One day a teacher tells her fourth-grade class, "Children, today we are going to start sex education. Now, the first subject I am going to discuss is *positions*. Do any of you children know any positions?"

Immediately a boy in the back of the room raises his hand and waves it frantically.

"Yes, Frankie?" she says.

"I know a *hundred* positions!" says little Frankie.

"Ahem, well ..." says the teacher a little nervously, "I don't think we have time to discuss a *hundred* positions right now, but if any of you children know just one or two ..." She looks around the room, but none of the children raises his hand.

"Well, I guess *I'll* start it off," says the teacher. "We'll begin by discussing the basic position, which is the woman on the bottom and the man on the top."

Suddenly little Frankie starts to frantically wave his hand again.

93

"Yes, Frankie?" says the teacher.

"*That*," says Frankie excitedly, "makes a hundred and *one*!"

* * *

Q: What do you call two gay guys named Bob?
A: Oral Roberts.

* * *

A man goes to the doctor because he is having some trouble. He hasn't had a bowel movement in over a week. The doctor recognizes the symptoms immediately and gives the man a prescription for some suppositories. He tells the man, "These should clear everything up. However, if there is still a problem after about a week, come back to see me."

A week goes by, and the man comes back in to see the doctor. He tells him that the problem is exactly the same, that it hasn't gotten any better at all. The doctor asks the man if he has been using the suppositories as prescribed.

"Yes, I have," says the man. "I've been taking three a day."

"*Taking* three a day?" says the doctor. "Have you been *eating* these things?"

"What do you think," asks the man sarcastically, "that I've been shoving them up my *ass*?"

* * *

Q: What do you call a Japanese Jew?
A: An Orienta.

94

A cab driver sees a woman hailing him at Thirty-ninth Street and Eleventh Avenue. He pulls over and is surprised when she gets in and sits down beside him on the front seat. She tells him her address and they drive off.

When they arrive at her destination, the cab driver pulls over and shuts off the meter.

"Okay," he says, "that will be four-sixty, please."

The woman looks over and says to him, "To tell you the truth, I don't have any money. But," she says, pulling her skirt up to her waist, "maybe *this* will take care of it."

The cabbie looks down and says, "Gee, lady, don't you have anything smaller?"

* * *

Q: What do you call four Mexicans drowning?
A: Quatro Sinko.

* * *

A man goes to his golf club and, hearing that his regular caddy will not be in that day, hires another caddy. The day goes along pretty well, and the new caddy seems quite knowledgeable. Upon arriving at a fairway that has always been particularly tricky for the golfer, the man turns to the boy and asks, "Which club do you think I should use for this shot?"

The caddy says, "Sir, I know this golf course very well. The best club for this fairway is the five iron."

The golfer gets out his five iron, lines up his shot,

and hits the ball. He smacks it really hard, and it veers way off to the right where his wife happens to be standing. It hits her in the head and she is killed instantly.

The wife is buried a few days later, and after the funeral, months and months go by before the man can even think about golf again. But after a year he thinks to himself, "I really loved the game. I shouldn't let it go out of my life. It was a freak accident. The game used to give me such joy, I should at least try to play once again and see how it feels."

He goes back out to the golf course, and as luck would have it, he gets the same caddy. When they get to that same fairway, he turns to the caddy and says, "Which club do you think I should use for this shot?"

The caddy says, "Sir, I know this golf course very well. The best club for this fairway is the five iron."

The man turns to the caddy and shouts, "You bastard! I played here a year ago and you told me to use the five iron and I *missed the green completely*!"

*   *   *

A young couple is living on a farm. One evening a flying saucer lands on the farm, right next to their house. Out of the flying saucer steps a young Martian couple, and they look very much like humans.

So the earth woman invites the Martians for dinner. They all sit down and start talking. They begin exchanging ideas and traditions, and they get to liking each other so much that they decide to switch partners for the night. The farmer and the Martian's wife go into one of the rooms, and the farmer's wife and the Martian man go into the other room.

As the Martian man takes off his pants the farmer's wife looks down and sees that his phallus is extremely small.

"What are you gonna do with that?" she says.

"I'll show you," he says, and proceeds to twist his right ear. Suddenly his penis extends to a foot and a half. However, it is still only as thick as a pencil.

"That's pretty long," says the woman, "but it's really not very wide."

The Martian then reaches up, twists his left ear, and he becomes as thick as a huge sausage. They then proceed to have sex.

The next morning, the Martians take off and the farmer and his wife are having breakfast.

"So, how was it?" says the farmer.

"It was great," says the wife, "the best sex I've ever had! How was yours?"

"Well," says the farmer, "it was kinda weird. All night long she kept playing with my ears."

*   *   *

Q: Why were the six Polish men pushing the house down the street?
A: They were trying to jump-start the oil burner.

*   *   *

A well-dressed gentleman with a slight Spanish accent got into my taxi one evening. When he told me that he was a psychiatrist, I told him that my father is a psychotherapist.

"Oh," said the man, "so you are put together well!"

I laughed and told him that my father is also a minister, and he said, "Oh, so you are put together very well!"

I laughed again and said, "Well, what about you? You're a psychiatrist! You must be put together well."

98

"Oh, no," said the man. "Shrinks are the worst! Shrinks are held together with Scotch tape!"

* * *

There are three big-game hunters in the jungle in Africa: an American, an Italian, and a Polish man. Suddenly they are captured by cannibals and brought before the chief. The chief tells them, "By tribal custom I am required to allow each of you a chance to escape, *and* I have to give you any weapon of your choice. However, I must warn you: If we catch you, we're going to skin you and make a canoe out of you." Before they even get a chance to get their breath, the chief points to the American and asks, "You're first, what do you want?"

The American says, "I want a gun."

The chief hands him a gun, and the American takes off into the jungle. Well, pretty soon the gun runs out of bullets and the natives catch up to him. They shoot him with poison darts, and within five minutes they skin him and make a canoe out of him.

The other two guys see this whole thing happen, and they look at each other. "Holy cow," one of them says to the other, "what are we going to do?"

The chief points to the Italian. "You're next. What do you want?"

The Italian says, "I want a horse."

The chief looks at him and says, "Well, that's not really a *weapon,* but if you want a horse, I'll give you a horse."

So the Italian rides off into the jungle. However, he is very quickly surrounded by a thousand natives on all sides, and he can't go anywhere. The natives shoot him with poison darts, skin him, and make a canoe out of him.

Finally the chief looks at the Polish guy. "What do *you* want?"

The Polish guy says, "I want a fork."

"A *fork*?" asks the chief. "What do you want a fork for?"

"Look," says the Polish guy, "you said I could have anything I wanted. Now give me a fork, all right? You'll see."

"Okay, okay," says the chief. "Here's the fork."

Immediately the Polish guy takes the fork and starts stabbing himself all over. The chief stares at him and exclaims, "What are you doing?"

The Polish guy laughs at him. "Ha, ha!" he says. "You're not going to make a canoe out of *me*!"

* * *

Q: Why do Jewish husbands die young?
A: They want to.

* * *

A huge, broad-shouldered mean looking hulk of a man is in a supermarket. He goes to the fresh produce section and tells the produce clerk that he wants to buy just half a head of lettuce.

"You can't do that," the clerk tells him.

But the man says, "Oh yeah?" and tears a head of lettuce in half. When he goes to the front to pay, the cashier tells him that he'll have to check with the manager before he can sell the man just half a head of lettuce.

So the cashier walks over to the store manager, and says, "Some big, dumb-looking asshole wants to buy half a head of lettuce." Just then the cashier notices that the huge man has followed him to the manager's office, is standing behind him, and just heard everything he said. Thinking quickly, the cashier points to the large man and tells the manager, "...and this kind gentleman has agreed to buy the *other* half."

A few days later the store manager tells the cashier, "I like someone who can think on his feet. In fact, I want to train you to become a manager, so I am sending you up to Winnipeg, Canada for a training seminar."

"Winnipeg, Canada?" the cashier responds with a grimace. "But the only people who come out of Winnipeg are either whores or hockey players!"

"I'll have you know," the manager says slowly, "that *my wife* is from Winnipeg!"

"Oh really?" the cashier responds. "What position does she play?"

* * *

Q: How did Staten Island get its name?
A: In the 1600s, when the Dutch first saw it from their ship, they kept saying to each other, " 'S dat an island?"

* * *

A Polish man said to me, "You know, you Americans have Polish jokes, but we in Poland tell American jokes. Would you like to hear an American joke from Poland?"

"Sure," I said.

"Okay," said the Pole. "How many Americans does it take to change a light bulb?"

I said, "I'll bite, how many?"

The Polish man said, "One."

* * *

Q: Why did God create Gentiles?
A: *Someone* has to buy retail.

* * *

Three men are stranded on a desert island: an Englishman, a Frenchman, and a Pole. They have been on the island for a year when they come across a lamp lying in the sand. They rub it and, of course, a genie appears.

The genie says to them, "Well, gentlemen, traditionally I give the person who finds the lamp three wishes. But, in this case, since there are three of you, I will give you each one wish."

The Englishman speaks right up. "I know what I want. I wish to be back in Piccadilly Circus in my favorite pub having a pint with all of my friends."

POOF! He disappears.

Next the Frenchman says, "I wish to be back in Paris in a nice little restaurant with a bottle of good wine and a beautiful woman by my side."

POOF! He disappears.

The Polish guy is sitting there thinking and thinking.

"And what would you like, my friend?" asks the genie.

"Gee, I don't know," says the Polish guy. "It's so hard to make up my mind. Boy, I sure wish those other guys were here to help me decide."

* * *

Q: Did you hear about the Polish actress?
A: She slept with the writer.

* * *

An American black man, an Italian, and a Polish man are sitting at a bar drinking together. At one point the bartender comes over to them. "You know," he says, "I'll bet a hundred dollars that there isn't twenty-five inches of dick among the three of you."

The three men look at each other, then at the bartender, then they all say, "You've got a bet!"

First the black guy stands up, lays his joint on the bar, and they measure him. He has twelve inches.

Next the Italian stands up and puts his dong out, and they measure him. He also has twelve inches.

The black and the Italian look at each other and smile until they look down at the Polish guy unzipping his trousers. As he puts his pecker on the bar all three men break out in a sweat.

He has one inch exactly, though, so they win the bet. The bartender gives them the hundred dollars, and they retire to a booth to divide up the money.

The Italian guy says, "Three doesn't go into a hundred evenly, so how are we going to split this up?"

The black guy says, "Well, since I was twelve inches, nearly half the amount we needed, I think I should get half of the money—fifty dollars."

The Italian guy says, "Well, I had twelve inches, too, so I think *I* should get fifty dollars."

"To tell you the truth, guys," says the Polish man, "I think *I* should get the whole hundred, because if I hadn't had a hard on, we wouldn't have won at all!"

* * *

Q: What's the difference between a proctologist and a bartender?
A: The proctologist looks at the assholes one at a time.

* * *

This guy walks into a bar and sits down next to a young woman. They start talking, and within a very short period of time, he tells her, "I'm divorced. My wife and I just couldn't get together sexually. I wanted to try new things, the latest ideas in sexual thinking, but she was very traditional. She just couldn't get into any of my new thinking."

The woman's eyes widen and she says, "That's funny, I've been divorced two years for the same reason, only my *husband* was traditional. *He* didn't want to try anything new sexually, and *I* was always looking for new ideas, new thinking. But he wasn't into it, so we got divorced."

So the guy says, "Hey, this is *great*. You and I are into the same thing! What do you say we go back to my place and get it on tonight?"

She says, "Great idea."

So they go back to his place, and he says, "Okay. Here's what I want you to do. Take off all your clothes, climb on my bed, get on your hands and knees, close your eyes, and count to six."

She says, "Great!" She takes off all her clothes, climbs on top of the bed, gets on her hands and knees, closes her eyes, counts to six, and nothing happens.

She says, "Six." Nothing happens. She says sweetly, "I'm waiting...."

The man then says, "Aw, jeez, I'm sorry. I got off already. I just shit in your purse."

*   *   *

A man is standing in line behind a woman at the bank. He looks down and notices that her dress is stuck between the cheeks of her rear end. So he reaches down and pulls it out. The woman turns around and says, "How dare you!" and slaps him in the face.

He says, "Sorry." And when the woman turns around again, he pushes it back in.

*   *   *

A young couple gets married. They are real country bumpkins, and on their wedding night they don't know what to do.

The man says to the woman, "Do you know what we're supposed to do tonight?"

"No," she says, "do you?"

"No, I don't," says the man. They sit there thinking until the husband says, "Wait a minute! Down in the shipyard there are a bunch of sailors. Sailors are supposed to know about these kinds of things. I bet we could get one of them to help us out!"

So he goes down to the dock and walks up to a sailor. "Excuse me," he says, "but my wife and I just got married today and we don't know what to do. Can you help us out?"

"Sure," says the sailor. "I have a little free time. I'll be glad to do what I can."

So the two men go back to the hotel room where the wife is waiting. The sailor takes one look at the beautiful wife and immediately says to the husband, "All right, here's what you should do." He then takes out a piece of chalk, and on the floor he draws a circle. He says to the groom, "Now you stand inside this circle and watch. No matter what I do, though, don't set foot outside the circle."

"Okay," says the man.

So the sailor goes over to the bed and makes love to the wife. When he's finished, he looks over at the husband standing inside the circle. The man is standing there giggling.

"What are you giggling about?" says the sailor.

The husband says, "I stepped out of the circle *twice*, and you didn't even notice!"

* * *

Q: What do a meteorologist in a snowstorm and a woman's sex life have in common?
A: They're both concerned with how many inches and how long it will last.

* * *

A woman places an ad in the Personals column of the newspaper. It reads, "Looking for a man who won't beat me, who won't run around on me, and who is a fantastic lover."

The woman waits a week but gets no reply. Then,

one day, her door bell rings. She goes to the door, opens it, and sees no one there. She closes the door and is about to walk away when the bell rings again.

She opens the door and once again sees no one there. Then she looks down and sees a man with no arms and no legs sitting on her doorstep. "I'm here to answer the ad," he says.

The woman doesn't know quite what to say, so the man continues, "You see, I can't beat you and I can't run around on you."

"Yes," says the woman, "but the ad also said that I wanted a fantastic lover."

The man looks up and says, "I rang the door bell, didn't I?"

* * *

Q: What's the difference between a porcupine and a Cadillac?
A: A porcupine has the pricks on the outside.

* * *

A little boy and a little girl are playing. The little boy pulls down his shorts and says, "*I* have one of these and you *don't*." The little girl starts crying and crying and runs home to her mother.

The next day the boy and girl are playing together again. Once again the boy points to his private parts and says, "*I* have one of these and you *don't*." But the little girl just keeps on playing. "How come," says the boy, "you're not *crying* today?"

"My mother told me," says the little girl, pulling

up her dress, "that with one of *these* I can get as many of *those* as I want."

* * *

A woman got into my cab one evening. "How are you tonight?" I asked.

She said, "I'd complain, but how long would you listen?"

* * *

A man is playing golf at a very exclusive country club for the first time, and on the eighth hole he hits a hole in one. So he walks down to the green, and as he takes his ball from the cup, a genie pops out.

"This is a very exclusive golf course," says the genie, "and it has everything, including the services of a genie if you make a hole in one in the eighth hole. I will be happy to grant you any wish you desire."

So the man says, "Great! I want to have a longer penis."

The genie says, "Your wish is granted!" and disappears down the hole.

So the golfer heads back to join up with his friends. As he is walking he can feel his penis slowly growing.

As the golf game progresses his penis keeps getting longer and longer until it comes out beneath his shorts and goes down below his knees.

He thinks to himself, "Hmmmm. Maybe this wasn't such a great idea after all." So he leaves his friends and goes back to the eighth hole with a bucket of balls and begins to shoot. Finally he shoots a hole in one, and by the time he gets down to the green, he has to hold his penis to keep it from dragging on the ground.

As he takes the ball from the cup, out pops the genie. "This is a very exclusive golf course," says the genie once again, "and it has everything, including the services of a genie if you make a hole in one on the eighth hole. I will be happy to grant you any wish you desire."

"Yeah, ' says the man. "Could you make my legs longer?"

* * *

Two days after Walter Mondale announced that Geraldine Ferraro would be his running mate, a man got into my cab and told me this one:

Q: What would be one of the best things about having a woman for vice-president?
A: We wouldn't have to pay her as much.

I couldn't wait to tell that one to a couple of friends of mine who are ardent feminists. I told it to them, of course, over the telephone, out of arm's reach!

* * *

A Jewish man and a Polish man are sitting at a bar, watching the news on the television. On the news they are showing a woman standing on a ledge, threatening to jump.

The Jewish man says to the Polish man, "I'll tell you what. I'll make a bet with you. If she jumps, I get

.wenty dollars. If she doesn't, you get twenty dollars. Okay?"

"Fair enough," says the Polish man.

A few minutes later the woman jumps off the ledge and kills herself. The Pole gets out his wallet and hands twenty dollars to the Jewish guy.

After about ten minutes the Jewish guy turns to the Polish guy and says, "Pal, I just can't take this twenty dollars from you. I have a confession to make. I saw this on the news earlier this afternoon. This was a repeat."

"No, no," says the Polish man. "You keep the money. You won it fair and square. You see, I saw this on TV earlier today too."

"You did?" says the Jewish guy. "Well, then, why did you bet that the woman wouldn't jump?"

"Well," says the Polish guy, "I didn't think she would be stupid enough to do it *twice*!"

*　　*　　*

Q: What do you call a man and woman using the rhythm method of birth control?
A: Parents.

*　　*　　*

A man goes into a bar and orders twelve shots of whiskey. The bartender lines up a dozen shot glasses on the bar, then fills them with whiskey. Quickly the man downs one after the other until he has finished all twelve.

"Well, pal," says the bartender, "what are you celebrating?"

"My first blow job," says the man.

"Oh, in that case," says the bartender, "let me buy you one more!"

"Nah," says the man, "if twelve won't get the taste out of my mouth, nothing will."

*   *   *

A man is walking down the street when he sees a man with four arms, and antennae coming out of his head. He goes up to him and says, "You're not from around here, are you?"

"No," says the man with the antennae.

"You know," says the man, "I don't think you're an *American*, either. As a matter of fact, I don't think you even come from this *planet*!"

"Right again," says the man with the four arms. "I'm from Mars."

"Well," says the man, "that's quite some configuration you've got there, with those four arms and those antennae and everything."

113

"Thank you," the Martian answers. "We Martians all have them."

"Well, that's just amazing," the man replies. "And, say, what is that big, round, gold plate there in your chest? I've never seen that before. Do all Martians have those?"

"Well, no," says the Martian, "Not the *goyim*."

*   *   *

A traveling salesman is in a small town in the Midwest for two weeks when he really begins to miss his wife. After another two weeks, he just can't take it anymore, and decides to visit the town brothel.

He goes up to the madam and says, "Here is a hundred dollars. Give me the worst blow job in the house."

"But sir," says the madam, "for a hundred dollars, you don't have to settle for the *worst* blow job. As a matter of fact, you could get the *best*."

"No, no," says the man, "you don't understand. I'm not horny, I'm *homesick*."

*   *   *

A Jewish man walks home every day past a pet shop. Each day as he passes he hears Hebrew singing coming from a parrot in the store. It sounds so beautiful that he feels happy for the rest of his walk home.

One day he decides that it would be really wonderful to have that beautiful singing fill his house. So he goes into the pet shop, buys the parrot and takes it home. The parrot sings him a Jewish prayer before dinner, and the man is very happy. It goes on like this for a few weeks, the bird singing happily for the man whenever he's home.

Upon the arrival of the Jewish high holy days, the man decides to take the bird with him to the temple. He makes the bird a little yarmulke and then walks happily to the temple. As he enters with the parrot on his shoulder his friend sees him.

"What? Moishe, you're bringing a bird *here*? To the temple? But, it's Rosh Hashanah!"

So the man replies, "Wait till you *hear* this bird! He know Hebrew and can sing all the prayers!"

"That's impossible, I don't believe you!" says the friend.

"You don't believe me?" says the man. "Fifty bucks says the bird can sing the prayers."

"You've got a bet," says the friend, and pulls out his money. The other men notice this, and pretty soon everyone is involved. Suddenly the man finds himself having bet a thousand dollars.

He turns to the bird and says, "Okay, bird, let's hear it!" But the bird just sits there. The man pleads, "Sing! Oh, please, sing!" But the bird is silent.

The rabbi says, "Time for the service!" And Moishe loses the bet.

Walking home, Moishe is fuming. "Boy! A thousand bucks! You sing *every day*! Why couldn't you at least have sung *one* little prayer?"

He gets home and takes out a knife. He starts sharpening it and says, "Okay, bird, I'm gonna have me a thousand-dollar parrot sandwich."

"Wait," says the bird.

"Wait for what?" asks Moishe.

"Wait till Yom Kippur," says the parrot. "We'll get ten-to-one odds!"

* * *

Little Red Riding Hood's grandmother is lying in her bed when the wolf bursts in through her door.

"Give me all your money," he demands, snarling and showing his teeth.

"Oh, no, you don't," says the grandmother, pulling a revolver out from under the covers and training it on the wolf. "You're going to *eat* me, like it says in the book!"

* * *

A man and his wife love to compete with each other. They are always racing each other to do things, betting each other. *Everything* is a contest. The husband, though, is beginning to get very depressed because he never wins. From the day they were first married, the wife has always won everything.

The man goes to a psychiatrist and tells him his problem. He explains that he wouldn't mind losing to his wife once in a while, but he has never won *anything*.

So the shrink says, "All we have to do is devise one game where you can't lose." He thinks for a moment, then says, "I've got it! Go home and challenge your wife to a pissing contest. Whoever can piss higher on the wall wins. Of course, you'll win. You're a man."

The husband goes home, runs in the house, and shouts upstairs, "Honey! Honey! I have a new game!"

She yells, "Oh, good! I love games," and runs down the stairs. "What is it?" she says.

He says, "Come outside." So they go out to the side of the garage. "Okay, look," he says. "We're both going to piss on the wall here, and whoever makes the higher mark wins."

The wife says, "Oh, good, good, good! I'll go first!" She then lifts up her leg, lifts up her dress, pees on the wall, and makes a mark about six inches high.

"Okay," he says, "Now it's my turn."

He unzips his trousers, takes himself out, and is just about to piss when his wife says, "Hey, wait a minute. No hands allowed!"

* * *

A guy walks into a drugstore and goes up to the pharmacist. "Last Friday I ordered twelve dozen rubbers, and when I got home, I found out I only got eleven dozen."

"Gee," says the pharmacist, "I hope I didn't spoil your weekend."

* * *

A woman has always been flat-chested, and she decides that she really wants to find out what it's like to have big breasts. She goes to a doctor, and he tells her, "The only remedy for this is to go to a witch doctor and ask him to marry you. If he says no, your bustline will grow."

So, figuring that she has nothing to lose, she sets out to find a witch doctor. She finds a really horrendous-

117

looking savage, but she goes up to him and says, "Witch doctor, will you marry me?"

He takes one look at her and says, "*NO!*"

Suddenly she grows two inches. Now, she's a thirty-four! She goes home, gets some new bras, and is very proud of her new figure.

She thinks, "That was so *easy*. Why don't I see what it's like to be a thirty-six?"

So the woman goes back the next week to the witch doctor and says to him, "Witch doctor, will you marry me?"

He looks at her and says, "I told you, *no!*"

She is now a thirty-six. She goes home, buys some new bras, and suddenly starts getting a lot of attention. She loves her new look and starts to think, "I wonder what it would be like to be a thirty-eight?" She has spent her whole life in a training bra, so she decides that she is ready to make up for lost time.

She goes back to the witch doctor and says, "Witch doctor, will you marry me?"

The witch doctor shouts at her, "*No! No!* A thousand times *no!*"

* * *

After I asked a man one night if he had heard any good jokes lately, he said, "Yeah! Here is one I told to my boss the other night at a cocktail party."

A very dapper, well-dressed gentleman walks into a midtown branch of the Chase Manhattan Bank one day and asks for a loan of $10,000 for two weeks.

The bank officer says to him, "Yes, sir, I think

we can arrange something. I'll just need some identification and credit references.''

"I'm sorry," says the very distinguished-looking man, "but I don't have either of those."

"Well, then," says the officer, "I'm afraid we can't help you."

"In that case," says the man, "I would like to speak to your boss."

He talks to the branch manager, who also tells him that a loan would be impossible. The man then demands to see someone higher up. This goes on and on, and the problem keeps getting kicked upstairs, until finally the man is ushered in to see David Rockefeller.

"Yes, sir," says Mr. Rockefeller, "what can I do for you?"

"I need a loan of $10,000 for two weeks," says the man.

"And do you have identification and credit references?" asks Mr. Rockefeller.

"No, I'm afraid I don't," says the man. "However, I am willing to put up my Rolls-Royce as collateral." With that, he produces the keys to his car and drops them on the desk. "It is parked right out front."

"Well," says Mr. Rockefeller, " a $150,000 car as collateral for a two-week $10,000 loan is good enough for me." The two men shake hands, and the man is issued the check.

One week later he returns. He goes up to the officer he first spoke with and says, "I would now like to repay my loan."

The officer, upon seeing the man, snaps to attention. "Sir," he says, "I have strict instructions that when you come in, I should send you in immediately to see Mr. Rockefeller."

The man is once again ushered in to see David Rockefeller. He sits down and pays back the loan with $200 interest. Once they have concluded their business, Mr. Rockefeller says to him, "Sir, from the license plate on your car, I was able to run a check on you. You are one of the the ten wealthiest men in the world! Why in the world would you want to leave your car here in exchange for a $10,000 loan?"

"Where else," says the man, "could I find such a great parking space so cheap?"

The man, upon finishing this joke, told me that when his boss heard it, his boss said to him, "Your timing is way off. You should have told me that joke two days ago. Yesterday I had lunch with David Rockefeller, and he would have loved it!" So, David, if it hasn't gotten back to you yet, I hope you're reading this now!

* * *

A man told me that he was walking along the street one day when he saw a blind man with a Seeing Eye dog walking along ahead of him.

"The light turned red," the man told me, "and I saw the dog stop. As they were standing on the corner waiting for the light to change, I noticed that the dog lifted his leg and pissed on the man's trousers. Then," said the man incredulously, "I saw the blind man reach into his pocket and give the dog a biscuit!

"At this point I had caught up with them, and as I was standing next to the man and his dog, waiting for the light to change, I couldn't resist asking, 'Excuse me, sir,' I said, 'but I just saw your dog piss on your leg. And *then* I saw you give him a dog biscuit!'

"The blind man turned toward me, and I swear he looked me straight in the eye, and said, 'I know that. I was just trying to find out where his head is, so I can kick him in the *ass*!'"

*   *   *

Why is it awful to be an egg?
1. You only get laid once.
2. The only one who ever sits on your face is your own mother.
3. It takes three minutes to get hard.
4. You come in a box with eleven others.

*   *   *

An old, retired couple is sitting at their kitchen table when the wife looks at the husband and says, "You know what? I feel like an ice cream. Will you go out and get me an ice cream?"

"All right, I'll get you an ice cream," says the man, getting up and putting on his coat.

"But, I don't want just *any* ice cream," says the woman, "I want a sundae."

"Okay," says the man, "I'll get you a sundae."

"But," the woman says, "I don't want just *any* sundae. I want a banana split. Do you want me to write this down for you?"

"No," says the man, "You want a special sundae; a banana split."

"Right," she says, "but not just *any* banana split. I want it to have a scoop of chocolate on one side and a scoop of vanilla on the other side. If you want, I'll write this down for you."

"I know what you want," says the man. "You want a special sundae; a banana split with a scoop of chocolate here, and a scoop of vanilla there."

"Yeah," she says, "but I want it to be *special*. I want it to have whipped cream on top. I'll write that down for you."

"No, no," says the man. "I know what you want. You want a special sundae; a banana split with a scoop of chocolate here, a scoop of vanilla there, and whipped cream on the top, right?"

"Yeah, but that's not good enough," says the old woman. "I want more. I want them to put some chopped nuts and a cherry on the top. I can write this down...."

"No, I *know* what you want," says the old man. "You want a special sundae; a banana split with a scoop of chocolate here, a scoop of vanilla there, some whipped cream, chopped nuts, and a cherry on top. Right?"

"Right!" says the woman.

Two hours later he comes back with a greasy paper bag. He puts it on the kitchen table and stands back. The woman walks over, opens the bag, looks inside, and sees four bagels.

She looks at him and says, "You forgot the cream cheese."

* * *

A man's father is very, very old, and the son can't afford very good treatment for him, so the old man is in a shabby, run-down nursing home. One day the son wins the lottery. The first thing he does is put his father in the best old age home money can buy.

His father is amazed at how beautifully run the place is. He can't get over it.

On the first day the old man is sitting watching TV, and he starts to lean a little bit to one side. Right away a nurse runs over and gently straightens up the old man. A little later the man is eating dinner, and when he finishes, he begins to tip a little bit to the other side.

Another nurse runs over and gently pushes him upright again.

The son calls his father that night and says, "Well, Dad, how are they treating you there?"

"It's a wonderful place," says the father. "The food is gourmet, they have color TVs in every room, the service is unbelieveable...."

The son says, "It sounds perfect!"

"It is," says the old man, "but there's just one problem. They won't let you fart."

*   *   *

Q: What do Italians call suppositories?
A: Innuendos.

*   *   *

About a hundred years ago a farmer is riding back from town with his horse and buggy. He pulls up alongside a friend of his who is also riding with a horse and buggy. They chat amiably for a few moments when suddenly the first man's horse leans his head over and bites the neck of the other horse.

The bitten horse rears up, and all the supplies fall off the other man's buggy. Both men stop and pick them up, and the first man apologizes profusely to his friend. After the friend rides off, the man walks around in front of his horse, looks him straight in the eye, and says, "That's *one*."

A little later the man is riding along when his horse, for no apparent reason, rears up, and all of *his* supplies fall off the buggy. So he stops, picks them all up, then walks around to the front of the horse. He

looks him straight in the eye and says, "That's *two*."

When the man arrives home, he gets down from his buggy and begins to tie the horse to the hitching post. As he is doing this the horse reaches over and bites the man on the shoulder. The man says, "That's *three*!" and runs into the house.

A few minutes later he comes out with a shotgun and *blam*! He kills the horse.

His wife hears the gun go off and runs out front. She sees what has happened and starts yelling at the man, "What have you done, you idiot? That was our only means of transportation! Now how are we going to get around? Oh, you bastard! You're just a hotheaded fool!"

The man turns to the woman and says, "That's *one*."

* * *

Q: Did you hear about the two gay Irishmen?
A: Gerald Fitzpatrick and Patrick Fitzgerald.

* * *

A born and bred New Yorker is in London. He is sitting by the Thames, taking in the sights, when a very proper English gentleman walks by.

"Excuse me, mista," says the New Yorker, "but can you tell me if dat's da Tower of London I'm lookin' at?"

"Sir," says the Englishman, "it is very improper to end your sentence with a preposition. Now, if you would care to rephrase the question, I would be glad to answer it for you."

"Uh, okay," says the New Yorker, "can you tell

me if dat's da Tower of London I'm lookin' at, *you asshole*?''

* * *

An American over in Japan contracts a strange Oriental venereal disease. He goes to many American doctors abroad, and they all give him the same grave news: He must have his penis amputated. In desperation he decides to see an Oriental doctor, in the hopes that he might know something more about his exotic disease.

"After all," he thinks to himself, "an Oriental doctor should know more about an Oriental disease."

So he goes to the doctor and asks, "Do *you* think I need to have my penis amputated?"

"No, no," says the doctor.

"No?" replies the man happily. "That's great! All the American doctors said they would have to cut it off!"

"Western doctors!" says the Oriental man. "All they ever want to do is cut, cut, cut! You see, all you have to do is wait two weeks. Then the penis will fall off by itself!"

* * *

Q: Why don't chickens wear underwear?
A: Their peckers are on their faces.

* * *

A married couple is having a really hard time making ends meet. They talk it over and finally decide

that in order to pay the rent and keep the family afloat, the woman will have to go out and sell herself.

So, one night she goes out and doesn't return until the wee hours of the morning. When she comes in, her clothes are all disheveled. She looks exhausted.

Her husband says, "You look like you've really been through it."

"Oh," says the woman, flopping down into a chair, "I have."

"Well," says the husband, "how much money did you make?"

The wife looks up with pride and says, "One hundred twenty-five dollars and twenty-five cents!"

"Twenty-five cents!" says the husband. "Who was the cheap bastard who gave you the twenty-five cents?"

"Why," says the wife, "*all* of them."

* * *

Q: What is this: 10, 9, 8, 7, 6, 5, 4, 3, 2, 1?
A: Bo Derek getting older.

* * *

Sidney Blumenfeld, age eighty-three, goes into the confessional at St. John's Cathedral. The priest asks him, "Have you anything to confess?"

"Yes," says the old man. "My wife died two months ago. Two days after she passed on I met another woman. This woman is twenty-two years old. I have been sleeping with her every day since the day I met her. Sometimes we do it two or three times a day."

127

"And *how* old are you?" asks the priest.

"Eighty-three," Sidney replies.

"Oh, dear!" says the priest. "Go home and say ten Hail Marys."

"I can't do that," says the old man. "I'm Jewish."

"Then for God's sake, why are you telling *me* all this?" asks the priest.

The old man replies, "I'm telling *everybody!*"

* * *

Q: What do you call a Greek with five hundred girlfriends?

A: A shepherd.

* * *

A young couple is having marital problems. They go to a marriage counselor, and he says to them, "First, we could start by discussing your sex life. For instance, how often do you make love?"

The young man says, "Well, Doctor, we make love every Monday, Wednesday, and Friday at ten o'clock."

"You mean," says the doctor, "that you make love *on schedule?*"

"Sure," says the man, "doesn't everybody?"

"No, no, no," replies the doctor. "Love is a very beautiful, spontaneous thing. When the feeling comes upon you, you've got to act on it. Be a little impulsive now and then. Now, go out this week," he continues, "and try to follow your feelings. Then come back next week and we'll discuss it."

The following week, when the couple comes in, they are holding hands, and the doctor can see that there

is a certain glow about them. They are smiling at each other, and they are acting a little shy. So the doctor says, "I see that it's been a special week for you. Would you care to tell me about it?"

"Well, Doctor," says the man, smiling and looking at his wife, "the day after we saw you we were having breakfast, and I looked across at her and she looked across at me, and before we knew it, we were making love right there on the table. It was very exciting!"

The doctor is so pleased for them. "That is wonderful," he says.

"Yeah," says the young man, "but I don't think they're ever going to let us into the Howard Johnson's again."

*   *   *

Two Martians flying through space are running low on rocket fuel. They happen to be passing near Earth, and one of them says, "Hey, there's life on that planet down there. Let's go down and try to get some fuel."

They fly down, and as luck would have it, they land in the middle of the desert in Nevada. They walk around for a while until they come to a road. After following the road for a couple of miles they come upon an old deserted gas station that has an old-fashioned pump with a round top.

One of the Martians walks up to the gas pump, pulls out his ray run, and says, "All right, Earthling, give me some fuel or I'm going to blast you."

The other Martian says to his friend, "Listen, man, don't hassle this guy. He's a bad dude. Let's get out of here."

"Nah," says the Martian, "I can handle him." Then, turning to the pump again, he says, "I'm giving you one last chance! Give me some fuel or I'll blast you!"

When the pump doesn't say anything, the Martian fires his ray gun at it. There is a huge explosion, and the Martians are blown into the sky and land two miles away in the desert.

The Martian with the ray gun looks at his friend and says, "Wow! You were right! That cat *was* a bad dude! How did you know he was so mean?"

"Well," says the other Martian, "I figured that any guy that could wrap his dick around his neck three times and then stick it in his ear, has *got* to be bad."

*　　*　　*

A ten-year-old boy goes into a house of ill repute. He goes up to the madam and says, "I want to buy a woman."

The madam says, "Get outta here. You're too young."

The kid reaches into his pocket and pulls out a huge wad of money.

"Well," says the madam, looking at the bills, "we *might* be able to work something out. What exactly did you have in mind?"

The little boy says, "I want a woman who has syphilis."

"Are you kidding me?" says the woman.

"Nope," says the kid. "I want a woman who has syphilis."

"Okay, it's up to you,' says the madam, picking up the telephone. She calls the worst place in town, and they send a woman over. The boy goes upstairs with the woman, has sex, and comes down and pays the bill.

"Thank you," he says, and starts to walk out.

"Wait a minute, wait a minute," says the madam. "Come here."

So the kid walks over to her. "Yes?" he says.

"I can understand you wanting to come in here," she says, "but I *don't* understand why you wanted a woman who has syphilis. Can you explain that to me?"

"Sure," says the kid "That means I got syphilis, right?"

She says, "Yeah . . ."

"And that means when I go home and get the maid tonight, that means *she'll* have syphilis too, right?"

"Right," says the madam.

"Then when the butler gets the maid, *he'll* get syphilis, right?"

"Right," says the madam.

"Then when the butler gets Mommy, *she'll* have syphilis, right?"

"Right," says the madam.

"Then, when Mommy gets Daddy, *he'll* have syphilis, right?"

"Right," she says.

"Then when daddy gets the gardener's wife, *she'll* get syphilis, right?"

"Right," says the curious madam.

"Then when the gardener's wife gets the gardener, *he'll* have syphilis, right?"

"Right," says the madam.

"Well, *that's* the jerk who killed my turtle."

*　　*　　*

132

A jazz musician's six-year-old son is plucking the petals from a daisy one by one, saying "She digs me; got no eyes; digs me; got no eyes . . ."

* * *

Two Polish men rent a rowboat and go fishing in a lake. They are catching fish after fish, and have almost two dozen by the end of the afternoon. One man says to the other, "Why don't we come back to the very same place tomorrow?"

"Good idea," his friend answers.

So the first man takes a piece of chalk, and draws an X on the bottom of the boat.

"Don't be stupid!" the friend says. "How do you know that we'll get the same boat tomorrow?"

* * *

A Polish guy is out hunting in the woods. Suddenly he comes upon a clearing, and there before his eyes is a beautiful, totally naked woman. She looks at him seductively and says, "I'm game!" So he shoots her.

* * *

An old Jewish couple is sitting in their living room after dinner. The husband is reading his evening newspaper when he turns to his wife and asks, "Vat is all dis here? Dis syphilis? Everybody gets dis syphilis! You can die! Vat is dis syphilis?"

His wife says, "Look, I tell you vat I'll do. I'll get de encyclopedia and look it up. Okay?"

So the husband sits there waiting until his wife comes back. She says, "You got nothing to vorry about."

"Vat do you mean, I got nothing to vorry about?" he says. "Is killing people, dis syphilis!"

"You got nothing to vorry about," says the wife. "According to de book, it only affects de Gentiles."

* * *

A Polish guy comes home early from work and finds another man in bed with his wife. He runs over to the dresser and pulls out a gun. He then puts it up to his own head.

When the wife starts laughing, the husband says to her, "Don't laugh, you're next."

* * *

A man goes into a bar and begins to tell a Polish joke. The man sitting next to him, a big, hulking powerhouse of a man, turns and says menacingly, "*I'm* Polish. Now you just wait a minute till I get my sons."

He then calls out, "Ivan! Come out here and bring your brother!"

Two men bigger than the first appear from the back room.

"Josef!" the man calls out, "you and your cousin come in here."

Two more men, the biggest of all, come in through the back door. All five men crowd around the man with the joke.

"Now," says the first Polish man, "do you want to finish that joke?"

"Nah," says the man.

"Oh, no? And why not?" says the Polish man, opening and closing his fist. "Are you scared?"

"No," says the man, "I just don't feel like having to explain it five times."

* * *

Q: What's the difference between a brownnoser and a shithead?

A: Depth perception.

* * *

A lion with a bad hangover is walking through the jungle early one morning. He is in an extremely grouchy mood, roaring at anyone who gets in his way. Suddenly he comes upon a giraffe.

"You know," says the lion to the giraffe, "you are *really* an ugly animal. Your neck is all out of proportion to your body, everybody has to strain his neck to talk to you, and you have those big ugly spots all over. Boy, are you awful to look at!"

The giraffe says to the lion, "Gee, I never thought of it that way, but, you know, you're right. I really *am* an eyesore. Look, I'm sorry, I'll move on out of your way so you won't have to look at me anymore."

With that, the giraffe shuffles away, totally depressed. Now the lion feels a little bit better, but he's still feeling grumpy, and soon he comes upon a hippopotamus.

"Now *you*," says the lion to the hippo, "are *really* ugly. I mean, you have those big ugly teeth, you're overweight, you have skin that is way too big for your body, and your skin is all cracked. Whew! Are you *grotesque*!"

The hippopotamus says, "Golly, I really can't argue with you. You're right. I'm sorry I have to spoil your view. I'll just push on so I won't cause you any more unpleasantness." And the hippopotamus walks slowly away, extremely depressed.

Now the lion feels quite a bit better. He's still a little testy, though, so in a few minutes, when he sees a frog, he says to the frog, "Of all the animals in the jungle, you look the *worst*. Man, are you disgusting! Your eyes bug out, they have a gross, slimy film all over them, and your skin is all covered with warts. Man, are you *revolting*!"

The frog looks at him and whines, "Fuck you! I've been sick!"

* * *

Q: What are a Jewish-American princess's first words?
A: Gucci, Gucci, Gucci.

* * *

A teacher announces to her class, "Children, the student who can name the greatest man who ever lived will win this shiny red apple."

Immediately an Italian boy raises his hand.

"Yes, Tony?"

136

"Christopher Columbus!" says Tony.

"Well," says the teacher, "Christopher Columbus *was* a very great man, but he wasn't the greatest man who ever lived."

Right away a little English girl raises her hand.

"Yes, Martha?"

"Winston Churchill," says the little girl.

"Well, no," says the teacher. "Although Winston Churchill was indeed a very great man, he wasn't the greatest who ever lived."

From the back of the room Little Bernie Goldstein raises his hand.

"Yes, Bernie?"

Bernie stands up and says, "Jesus Christ."

"That is *correct*, Bernie," says the teacher. "Come up and collect your apple."

When Bernie gets up to the front of the room, the teacher hands him the apple. "You know, Bernie," she says, "given the fact that you're Jewish, I'm surprised you said that *Jesus* was the greatest man who ever lived."

"Well, actually," says Bernie, "I *do* think *Moses* was the greater man, but business *is* business."

* * *

Q: What does a dog do that a man steps into?
A: Pants.

* * *

Two men are out camping. They are sleeping in their tent when one of them cries out in pain. The other man wakes up just in time to see a deadly, poisonous snake slithering out of the tent.

"That snake just bit me right on my cock!" cries the man. "Hurry! Run and call a doctor to see what we should do!"

Without a moment's hesitation the other man springs from the tent and runs two miles through the woods to a campsite where there is a pay phone. He calls a doctor, and though he is totally out of breath, he manages, in gasps, to tell the doctor what has happened.

"What should I do, Doc?" he asks.

The doctor says, "Listen carefully. You must go back to your friend and with a razor blade cut an *X* right on the spot where the snake bit him, then suck out the venom. But do it quickly or your friend will die!"

The man runs two miles back through the forest and arrives at the tent. His friend looks up anxiously and says, "What did the doctor say?"

The man tells him, "You're gonna die."

* * *

Q: What's a Polish cocktail?
A: Perrier and water.

* * *

Two men die and arrive in heaven. They walk up to St. Peter at the pearly gates and give him their names.

"Gentlemen," says St. Peter, "there seems to be a slight problem. Heaven happens to be completely full right now, and I'm afraid you won't be able to come in for a couple of weeks.''

"What?" say the two men. "That can't be! We were good all our lives! We should be able to come into heaven right now!"

"Well," says St. Peter, "we'll make it up to you. You two men can go back to earth for two weeks as anything you like. And when there is room up here, we'll come down and get you and you can come right in."

The two men are in agreement that this seems to be an equitable arrangement, and so when St. Peter asks them what they would like to be, the first man steps up and says, "I have always wanted to fly, so I would like to return to earth as an eagle in Colorado."

"It is done," says St. Peter, and the man disappears. "Now," he says, turning to the other man, "what would you like to be?"

"I," says the man, "would like to be a stud in L.A." And with that, he disappears.

A couple of weeks later St. Peter summons one of the angels. "Well," he says to the angel, "we have some room up here now, and I would like for you to go down and get those two gentlemen we had to send back to earth."

"Fine," says the angel, "but how will I find them?"

"Well," says St. Peter, "the first one shouldn't be too hard to find. There aren't too many eagles in Colorado, so just look for the one flying the highest, and that is bound to be him."

"All right," says the angel. "And the second man?"

"Now, the second man," says St. Peter, "might be a little trickier to find. There have been a lot of building projects in Los Angeles lately."

* * *

One night while I was driving my cab I was in an accident. I was taken to the hospital and was pronounced clinically dead for five minutes before I was revived. During the time I was "dead," I went to heaven, and I clearly remember what it was like. I was walking around checking out everything, and I saw a large wall with hundreds of clocks on it. But, oddly, the clocks had only minute hands, and they would jump at irregular intervals. An angel happened to be passing by, and I asked her what these clocks were for.

"Oh," she said, "that's how we keep track of how often people masturbate on earth."

I looked more closely, and sure enough, under each clock there was a little nameplate. So I had a marvelous time looking up all the people I knew. But after a few minutes I said to the angel, "Wait a minute, I don't see my best friend Carl Smith's name here."

The angel said, "Oh, yes. They keep that one over in the office. They're using it for a fan."

*   *   *

Q: What do you call a lesbian eskimo?
A: A Klondyke.

*   *   *

A guy is driving down the road in Italy on his way to Salerno. By the roadside he sees a car broken down with a man and woman standing beside it. He pulls over and gets out of his car to see if he can help. Suddenly the man pulls a gun on him.

"All right, buddy," says the man, "I want you to jerk off."

"What?" he says.

"Go ahead, do it," says the man, holding the gun to the guy's head.

So the guy masturbates, and when he is through, he says, "All right. Can I go now?"

"No, I want you to do it again," says the man.

"Again?" the man exclaims. "I just did it."

"Do it again."

So he does it again. It takes him a little longer this time, but when he is finished, he says, "Now can I leave?"

"One more time. I want you to do it again."

The guy is really scared now; he's starting to sweat. It takes him quite a long time, but finally he comes a third time.

"Now can I leave?"

"Yeah," says the man, lowering his gun, "and this is my sister. I want you to drive her into Salerno."

* * *

Q: What is six inches long that women love?
A: Money.

* * *

A man with a poodle goes into a bar. After ordering a drink he tells the bartender that he would like to buy some cigarettes, but the bartender replies that, unfortunately, they have run out. So the man says, "That's all right, I'll just send my dog across the street to get some."

He searches through his pockets for the money and discovers that the smallest bill he has is a twenty. He puts it in the dog's mouth and tells the dog, "Boy, run across the street and get me some cigarettes, and don't forget to bring back the change."

Immediately the poodle runs out the front door. A man sitting at the bar says to the dog's owner, "Say, that dog is really something! Is he really going to bring cigarettes back to you?"

"Sure," says the man. "He can do all sorts of stuff. He is an amazing dog."

Just then they hear the loud sound of tires screeching. The man looks up with fear in his eyes and says, "Oh, no!" He runs out to the street and sees a car stopped in front of the bar.

When he runs around to the front of the car, he sees that it did not hit his dog after all but managed to

143

stop just in time. The reason, however, for the sudden stop was to avoid hitting the dog who was humping another poodle right in the middle of the road.

"Hey," says the man to his dog, "what's going on? You never did anything like this before!"

The dog looks up and says, "I never had twenty dollars before."

* * *

A family got into my cab one evening, a husband, his wife, and their teenaged daughter. As we exchanged jokes for a while I was, of course, limiting my selections to only clean ones.

When I got them to Tavern on the Green, the man, sitting nearest the door, got out first, then the daughter. As the wife slid across the backseat to get out, she paused a moment to lean over and say quietly into my ear, "Do you know why the Polish man didn't enjoy his honeymoon?"

"No," I said.

"Because he was waiting for the swelling to go down," she said before getting out and rejoining her family.

* * *

A little boy goes up to the counter in a drugstore and asks the clerk for a box of Tampax. The clerk puts them into a paper bag and says to the boy, "Are these for your mommy?"

"No," says the boy.

"Well, then," says the clerk, "are they for your sister?"

"Uh-uh," says the boy.

"Well, then," says the clerk, "who are they for?"

"They're for me," says the boy.

"For you?" says the surprised clerk. "What are you going to do with them?"

"I don't know yet," says the boy. "All I know is that I keep seeing on TV that if you buy these, you can go horseback riding, swimming, camping..."

*   *   *

Q: What's the difference between a pig and a fox?
A: About four drinks.

*   *   *

A flea is on the beach in Florida. He's got his little beach chair and is sunbathing with his little reflector when a friend of his happens to walk by. The other flea looks really beat up, all disheveled and mussed. The flea catching the rays looks up and says, "Hey, what happened to you? You look terrible."

"Oh," says the other flea, "I had an *awful* trip down here. I hitched a ride in a guy's mustache, and how was I to know he was coming down on a motorcycle? It was just terrible! The wind was blowing me all over the place, bashing me around! I had to hold on for dear life!"

"Well," says the flea sitting in the sun, "you did it the wrong way. What you have to do next time is go to the *airport*, and go to the stewardesses' lounge. Then you hop up on the toilet seat, and when one of the stewardesses sits down, you jump up into her pubic

...air. It's warm, it smells good, and you ride down in style. Try it *that* way the next time!"

So, the next year, the same flea is on the beach with his little reflector, catching some rays when he looks up and sees his friend. The other flea is again all mangled and beaten up.

"Hey," he says, "what happened to you? Last year I thought I told you how to make this trip the *right* way."

"Yeah, well," says his friend, "I went to the airport, like you said. I went to the stewardesses' lounge. I hopped up on the toilet seat. A stewardess sat down. I jumped up in her pubic hair. The next thing I knew, I was in this guy's mustache on a motorcycle."

* * *

Q: What are the three biggest lies in the music business?
A: 1) Your check is in the mail.
   2) We'll fix it in the mix.
   3) I won't come in your mouth.

There is also a fourth lie (This one is for all you New York free-lance musicians):

4) If you do the tour, you'll play on the album.

* * *

Q: What are two unfulfilled Polish promises?
A: "The check is in your mouth," and "I won't come in the mail."

* * *

One night a man told me that he was a trader of stocks and bonds. I asked him how he liked it, and he said, "It's all right as long as you don't see too much red ink. I am the only person I know whose favorite color is black."

I said to him, "You know, I don't really understand what a bond is. Could you explain it to me?"

"A bond," said the man, "is something like a promissory note on a loan."

"Oh," I said.

As we pulled up to his destination he said, "Let me put it this way: Do you have any stocks?"

"No," I said.

"Do you have any debts?" he asked.

"Yes," I replied.

"That's the difference," he said as he handed me the fare and got out of the cab.

I sat there for a few moments scratching my head

*   *   *

A farmer has a rooster that goes around screwing all the animals in the barnyard. The rooster keeps this up for quite a while before the farmer finally pulls him aside and warns him. "Look," the farmer says, "you had better take it a little easier or you're liable to screw yourself to *death*."

The rooster just laughs at the farmer and goes out and has all the chickens in the chicken coop. He then goes through all the cows, then the pigs, and so on, until he has been with all the animals on the farm.

He keeps this up every day for weeks. Then one day the farmer doesn't see the rooster around the barnyard, so he goes looking for him. Out above one of his fields, the farmer sees some vultures circling around and around. The farmer runs out and sees the rooster lying spread-eagled on the ground.

"I knew it!" says the farmer. "I knew this would happen to you! Oh, why didn't you listen to me when I warned you?"

The rooster opens one eye, points upward, and says, "Shhh. They're getting lower."

* * *

A man living near the Bronx Zoo wakes up one morning and looks out the window. There, sitting in a tree in his backyard, is a big gorilla. In a panic he looks in the yellow pages for gorilla exterminators and finds one listing. He quickly dials the number, and when a man answers, he shouts, "Please hurry! I have a gorilla in a tree in my backyard!"

When the exterminator pulls up in front of the man's house, the man runs out excitedly, telling him that the gorilla hasn't moved at all. So the exterminator says, "Good. Help me unload the truck."

The exterminator takes out of the truck a ladder, a baseball bat, an English bulldog, a large piece of rope, and a shotgun. They take all this stuff around to the side of the house, and just before they round the corner to the backyard, the exterminator stops.

"Okay," he says to the man, "you're going to

have to help me with this. Now, I've done this many times before and there's never been any problem, but you must listen very carefully.''

"First I'm going to go around to the other side of the tree, behind the gorilla, put the ladder against the tree, and climb up. Next I'm going to hit the gorilla with the baseball bat and knock him out of the tree. Now, you will be holding this English bulldog by the leash. When the gorilla hits the ground, you let go of the leash. This English bulldog has been specially trained to do one thing and one thing only. He will run up to the gorilla and bite the gorilla's balls off. This will stun the gorilla, and while he is in this state of shock, you and I will run up with the large piece of rope, tie up the gorilla, and load him into the back of my truck. You got it?"

"Yes," said the man.

"Now, it's very important that we do everything in the proper sequence, so I want you to repeat the entire procedure back to me."

"Okay," says the man. "First you climb up the ladder behind the gorilla, then you hit the gorilla with the baseball bat, knocking him out of the tree. When he hits the ground, I let go of the specially trained English bulldog and he will run up and bite the gorilla's balls off. This will stun the gorilla, and while he is in this state of shock, we run up with the large piece of rope, tie up the gorilla, and load him into the back of your truck."

"Okay. You got it," says the exterminator. "Let's go."

He is just about to start to move toward the tree when the man says, "Wait a minute! What's the shotgun for?"

"Oh, yeah," says the exterminator, "I almost forgot to tell you. That's the most important part! Now, this is just a precaution—it has never happened before—but in the event that the gorilla should somehow knock *me* out of the tree, shoot the dog."

*   *   *

Q: What do you call initials on an Italian's fingers?
A: A monogrammed handkerchief.

*   *   *

A well-known modern artist is commissioned to do his interpretation of Custer's Last Stand. He spends months on the painting, and when he is finished, a big ceremony is held for the unveiling.

The press is all there, as well as a number of government officials. The leaders of the art world and high society are also present, eagerly awaiting the big moment. Finally, all the distinguished guests are seated, and the sheet is drawn back, bringing the canvas into full view. A shocked silence falls upon the room.

There, in the center of the painting, is a large cow with a halo over its head. Surrounding the cow, from the foreground to the background, are hundreds of copulating Indians.

No one in the hushed room knows how to react until finally one member of the press corps stands up and addresses the artist. "Sir," he says, "could you possibly explain the imagery in your painting to those of us not well educated in modern art?"

"All right," says the artist. "You see, my painting represents my conception of what was going through

General Custer's mind at the exact moment he came over the hill at Little Big Horn. I believe that his very first thought was, 'Holy cow, look at all those fucking Indians!'"

*　　*　　*

Q: What does a man do standing up that a woman does sitting down and a dog does on three legs?
A: Shake hands.

*　　*　　*

One day while Prince Charles and Lady Diana were in the United States the Prince went to attend a pro basketball game. After the game he visited the locker room because he wanted to congratulate Kareem Abdul-Jabbar on a magnificent performance. As Prince Charles spoke to him Kareem was getting dressed, and the Prince happened to look down, noticing something quite startling. "Wow," he said, "that's quite some *size* you have there, Kareem. That must run in the family, eh?"

"No, not at all," said Kareem. "There's a trick to it. Do you want to know what it is?"

"Sure!" said Prince Charles.

"Well," said Kareem in a confidential tone, "just before you go to bed at night, you take out your thing and whack it on the bedpost three times. In no time at all you'll be surprised at how big it has gotten."

"Gee, thanks a lot!" said the Prince, and hurried home to try it out. When he got there all the lights were turned out, so to avoid waking Diana, he got undressed in the bathroom. He then quietly walked over to the bed, took out his member, and whacked it on the bedpost three times.

Lady Di's voice suddenly came out of the darkness. "Kareem, is that you?"

* * *

Q: Why do farts smell?
A: So deaf people can enjoy them too.

* * *

A man is sitting in a café in Mexico, trying to decide what he wants to order, when a waiter walks by On the plate he is carrying are two big round hunks of meat, about the size of grapefruits.

The man calls the waiter over, points to the plate and says to him, "*That's* what I want!"

"I'm sorry, sir, but that is the special, and there is only one order of the special available each day."

"Well, what kind of special is that?" asks the man.

"You see, sir," says the waiter, "those are the balls of the bull killed today in the bullfight. It is our most popular item, and one must reserve it many days in advance."

"When is the next free day?" asks the man.

The waiter checks his book and says, "Tuesday.

"All right, then, " says the man, "put me down for Tuesday."

So each day the man eats at the café and sees the huge bull balls being delivered to the eagerly waiting customer.

Finally Tuesday arrives, and the man excitedly goes to the café and sits at his regular table. "I'd like the special, please," he says, and sits back, anticipating a wonderful meal.

When the waiter arrives, though, on the plate there are just two small pieces of meat hardly larger than grapes.

"Hey, what is this?" says the man.

"I'm sorry, sir," says the waiter, "but you see, the bull doesn't *always* lose."

* * *

Q: What do you need when you have three lawyers up to their necks in cement?

A: More cement.

* * *

A man decides that he wants to become a monk. So he goes to the monastery on the hill and asks to see the head monk. He is taken in to see the man and is informed that before he can become a monk, he must pass two tests.

"First," says the head monk, "we will put you in a cell for six months. You will have nothing to eat or drink but bread and water, and each entire day must be spent reading the Bible."

"Then," he continues, "should you pass the first test, you will be ready for the second test. For this we put you in a room and take off all your clothes. We then tie a little bell to your male member, and then we walk a nude nun through the room. Should that little bell make any sound at all, I'm afraid you will be deemed unfit to join the monastery."

"Now," says the monk, "do you think you can pass these two tests?"

"I can," says the man.

So they put him in a cell with nothing but bread and water, and he does nothing but read the Bible all day and night for six months. At the end of this time he is once again brought before the head monk.

"Sir," he says, "I have successfully completed the first test."

"Are you ready for the second?" asks the head monk

"I am," says the man.

He is taken into a room and stripped down. They put the little bell on him, then they walk a nude nun through the room. Well, right away his bell starts ringing.

The monk says to him, "I'm sorry, but I'm afraid you must leave."

"Wait a minute," says the man. "Are you going to tell me that *every* priest in this monastery has passed this test?"

"Every one," says the monk.

"Before I will agree to leave," says the man in defiance, "I demand proof. I want to see *ten* monks pass this test."

"All right," says the monk.

They get ten monks in the room, undress them, line them up, and put bells on them. The nude nun then walks through and there is nothing but dead silence.

Except, of course, for the first man's bell, which is ringing like crazy. As a matter of fact, it gets to ringing

156

so hard, it falls off. When the man bends over to pick it up, all of the other ten bells ring.

*   *   *

Q: Why couldn't Mozart find his teacher?
A: He was Haydn.

*   *   *

A man walks into a bar and he has this little guy sitting on his shoulder.

"Let me have a Scotch," says the man.

The bartender gives him a Scotch, and before the man can drink it, this little guy runs down the man's arm and *bam*! kicks the drink across the room.

"Oh, I'm terribly sorry," says the bartender, "here, let me give you another one."

He gives the man another Scotch, and just as the man is about to pick it up, the little man runs down his arm and *bam*! kicks it across the room again.

"Hey, what's going on?" asks the bartender.

"Just give me another Scotch," says the man, glowering.

"Okay," says the bartender, and gives him another one.

Once again, before he can drink it, the little man runs down his arm and *bam*! kicks the Scotch across the room.

158

"Hey, look, fella," says the bartender, "what is this? Who is this little guy here? What's going on?"

"All right, I'll explain," says the man. "You see, I'm an astronaut, and on one of my flights the capsule I was in got lost and I was on a deserted island for a little bit. I was walking on the beach when I happened to stumble on this antique lamp half buried in the sand. I picked it up and rubbed it, and a genie appeared. She said I could have anything I wanted, so I asked for a twelve-inch prick. And here he is."

*   *   *

Two old Jewish men are sitting on a park bench. One of them says, "Today is the proudest day of my life. Today my son graduated from law school."

The other man says, "N.Y.U.?"

The first man says, "And why not?"

*   *   *

A Polish man wants lunch, so he goes down the street to a place he knows of, walks up to the counter, and says, "I want a burger, some fries, and a chocolate shake."

The man behind the counter says, "You must be Polish."

The guy says, "Oh, I can't believe it! Everyone *always* knows," and he storms out of the place. He vows that he is going to learn to disguise his Polishness if it's the last thing he ever does.

He goes to a school to lose his accent. He goes to a fashion designer to have a whole new wardrobe designed for him. Then he goes to a finishing school to learn all the proper manners and how to behave in all circumstances.

A couple of months later the Polish man goes back to the same place and goes up to the same man at the counter.

"I would like to start first with some vichyssoise," he says, "then I'll have some steak tartare, and then I think I'll finish it all off with some fresh raspberries."

The man behind the counter says, "You must be Polish."

The guy freaks out. "I just spent thousands of dollars on a wardrobe and finishing school! How is it that you *always* know I'm Polish?"

"Because," the man behind the counter says, "this is a hardware store."

160

Q: Did you hear about the new restaurant on the moon?

A: Great food but *no* atmosphere.

* * *

A Jewish man, a Polish man, and a man from India are driving around looking for a hotel. Unfortunately a convention happens to be in town that night, and there are no rooms available.

They wind up driving to the outskirts of the city where at last they come across a motel with a VACANCY sign. They stop and go in to register.

"I'm sorry," says the clerk, "but we only have one room left and it's only a double."

The three men explain how desperate they are, and so the clerk says, "Okay. I know what we can do. One of you men can sleep out in the barn. Don't worry, though, we'll put a cot out there and make it nice and comfortable for you."

The clerk then shows them to their room, and as he is leaving he says, "It's just up to you three to decide who is going to sleep in the barn."

Without hesitation the man from India says, "No problem. I'll sleep in the barn."

He leaves, and a few minutes later, as the other two men are getting ready for bed, they hear a knock on the door. They open it, and the Indian man is standing there. "So sorry," he says, "I cannot sleep with the sacred cow."

"So I'll sleep in the barn," says the Jewish man, and he leaves. A few minutes later the other two men hear a knock on the door. They answer it, and the Jewish guy is standing there. He shrugs and says, "Can't sleep with the pig."

So the Polish guy says, "I guess I'll sleep in the barn."

He leaves. The Indian and the Jewish man are beginning to undress when they hear a sound at the door. They open it and the pig and the cow are standing there.

*　　*　　*

Q:　Did you hear about the new gay Chinese restaurant?
A:　The most popular dish there is Sum Yung Gai.

*　　*　　*

A young priest happens to get a seat next to an old rabbi on the airplane they are taking across the country.

While waiting on the runway the priest begins talking to the rabbi.

"You know," he says, "you really should think about becoming a Roman Catholic. It is the best religion of all, chosen in the eyes of God!"

As the plane takes off the eager young priest continues, trying to talk the old rabbi into joining the Roman Catholic faith. Suddenly the plane goes into a tailspin and crashes. The priest is miraculously thrown from the plane. As he looks back at the wreckage he sees the old rabbi pick himself up and make the sign of the cross.

The priest runs up to him, saying, "Oh, thank heavens I got to talk to you in time. In the heat of the moment, as we were going down, you saw that what I was saying was right and you decided to convert!"

"Vat are you talking about?" asks the old rabbi.

"As you stepped from the wreckage," says the priest, "I saw you make the sign of the cross!"

"Vat cross?" says the rabbi. "I vas checking: spectacles, testicles, vallet, vatch."

*   *   *

A guy got into my cab one day, and after speaking with him for a few minutes, it turned out that we both play drums. After exchanging several musician jokes he told me this one:

Four guys are sitting at a bar, two at one end and two at the other. The first two men begin talking to each other, and their conversation starts with computers, then continues on to politics and world affairs. When the discussion turns to the stockmarket, one of the two men says to the other, "You know, I really like you. What's your IQ?"

The second man says to the first, "It's 135. What's yours?"

"It's 140. No wonder we get along so well. Say, what do you say we leave this place and go to that lecture on nuclear physics?"

"Great!" says the other man. "Let's go!"

As they leave, the two other men at the far end of the bar are sitting with their beers in front of them and their heads hanging.

The first one says to the other, "Did you hear that?"

"Yeah," says the second man.

"What's *your* IQ?" says the first one.

"Twenty-five," says the second.

"Mine's thirty," says the first one. "What size sticks do you use?"

A true drummer's joke, or so I thought. Since then, however, I have heard this joke told many times in many variations, from guitarists ("What size strings do you use?") to actors ("Been to any auditions lately?").

* * *

Q: How do you know that Jesus was Jewish?
A: He lived at home till he was thirty, he went into his father's business, he thought his mother was a virgin, and she thought he was God.

* * *

164

A young couple get married, and they've never made love before. On their wedding night the wife is quite anxious to get things going, but the man seems to be having some difficulty. Finally he starts to undress, and when he takes off his pants, she notices that his knees are deeply pockmarked and scarred. So the wife says, "What happened to you?"

The man says, "Well, when I was very young, I had the kneesles."

He then takes off his socks, and his wife sees that his toes are all mangled and deformed.

"I don't understand," she says. "What happened to your feet?"

"Well, you see," says the man, "when I was a young boy, I had tolio."

So then the man takes off his shorts and the woman says, "Don't tell me. Smallcox."

* * *

Two leprechauns knock on the door of a convent. A nun answers and says, "How can I help you, little fellows?"

"Have you got any midget nuns?" asks one of the leprechauns.

"Midget nuns?" she says. "No, I'm sorry, we don't."

The leprechaun says, "Oh, come on, you've got at least *one* midget nun."

"I'm sorry, little man," she tells him, "but I'm afraid we don't."

The leprechaun starts to get worked up and pleads with her, "Please!" he says, "you've got to tell me that you have at least one midget nun!"

Finally his friend, the other leprechaun, elbows him in the ribs. He says, out of the side of his mouth, "You see, Darby, I *told* you it was a penguin you screwed."

* * *

Q: What's the difference between a light bulb and a pregnant woman?
A: You can unscrew the light bulb.

* * *

An elephant is walking through the jungle and accidentally falls into a hole. The elephant, try as he might, cannot get out, and so he lets out a loud roar. A little mouse is walking nearby and hears the sound, so he goes over to investigate. There he finds the elephant stuck in the hole.

"Hang on," he says to the elephant. "I'll get my friends and we'll help you out."

The little mouse runs and gathers all his friends together. They all go back to the hole and climb down into it. The elephant tries to get up, and the little mice all push as hard as they can, but they are just too small to push the big elephant out.

The first little mouse says to the elephant, "It's okay, don't worry. I know what I can do. I'll just go get my *Porsche*."

"You have a *Porsche*?" says the incredulous elephant.

"Oh, yeah," says the mouse, "everybody's getting them. Haven't you heard? Hang on, I'll be right back." So he runs off.

A few minutes later he comes back, driving his Porsche. He backs it up to the edge of the hole, the elephant curls his trunk around the bumper, and the mouse easily pulls him out.

After receiving many thanks the mouse drives off, and the elephant goes on his way.

A few weeks later the mouse falls into a hole. He can't get out because the sides are too steep, so he cries out for help. Who should be passing by at that moment but the elephant he helped a few weeks earlier.

"I'll get you out," says the elephant, and puts his foot into the hole. But his foot is just too wide for the mouse to grab. Next the elephant tries his trunk, but it is too slippery.

Finally the elephant says, "I have an idea. Here's what we can do. I have a very large penis. I'll masturbate, and when I get hard, the tip of my penis will come out through the foreskin. When that happens, the tip will be dry. You can grab on to it, and I will pull you out."

"Okay," says the mouse.

Sure enough, everything happens just as the elephant said it would, and the little mouse is saved.

And what is the moral of the story?

If you have a big cock, you don't need a Porsche.

* * *

Q: How many surrealists does it take to change a light bulb?
A: A fish.

* * *

A woman is in a pet store and goes up to the owner. "Excuse me, sir," she says, "I'm looking for a pet. I want something really special, something unique. Do you have anything that might fit that description?"

"I have just the thing you're looking for," says the owner, and he disappears into the back room. He returns a moment later, carrying a carved ivory box. He places it on the counter and ceremoniously lifts off the top. The woman looks in, and there, sitting quietly, is a frog.

"This, madam," says the store owner, "is no ordinary frog. *This* frog has been specially trained in the art of cunnilingus."

The woman is immediately interested. Although momentarily taken aback by the two-thousand-dollar price tag, when assured by the owner that this frog is indeed an expert in his field, she plops the two thousand dollars down on the counter. She puts the carved ivory top back on the box, picks it up, and leaves the store, a smile playing across her lips.

The woman gets home, takes a bath, puts on some perfume, and lies down naked in her bed. She takes the frog out of the box and puts it on the bed between her legs.

She waits and she waits and nothing happens. The frog just sits there. Angrily she picks up the phone and calls the pet store.

"I just paid two thousand dollars," she shouts, "and this frog is doing absolutely nothing!"

"I'll be right over," says the owner.

So the owner arrives, and they put the frog on the bed again, but the frog just sits there. They wait and wait and nothing happens.

Finally the owner says to the frog, "All right, now, *watch*, 'cause this is the *last time* I'm going to show you!"

* * *

One day a little polar bear cub says to his mother, "Mommy, am I really a polar bear?"

"Why, certainly you are, dear," she says. "You live on the North Pole and you swim under the ice to catch fish. You do fun things like playing on ice floes and romping through the snow to catch seals. *Of course* you're a polar bear. Why do you ask?"

"Because," says the little cub, "I'm fucking *freezing!*"

* * *

A man takes his wife to the zoo. They are standing all alone in front of the gorilla cage, and the man says to his wife, "You know, honey, why don't you take off your blouse? I want to see how the gorilla will react."

"What?" says the woman. "Are you out of your mind?"

"Look, there's no one else around," says the man. "Just take off your blouse."

The woman takes it off, and the ape starts going a little crazy, running back and forth in the cage.

"Okay, sweetheart," says the husband, "why don't you take off your bra?"

"No," she says.

"There's no one else around," he says. "Please take off your bra."

So she takes it off, and the gorilla begins to jump up and down and run faster back and forth across the cage.

"Now," says the husband, "take off your skirt."

"This is a public place!" says the woman. "I'm not taking off my skirt!"

"There's no one else here!" he says.

"We're in a zoo!" she protests.

"Just do it," says the husband.

Finally she undresses, and the ape goes really wild. He starts making noises, beating his chest, and then he starts rattling the bars of the cage.

With this, the man opens the door to the cage, shoves his wife in, closes the door, and says, "*Now,* I want you to tell *him* you have a headache."

* * *

Q: What's the difference between like and love?
A: Spit or swallow.

* * *

Two space scientists at Cape Canaveral are about to test a new rocket fuel when they notice a strange condensation on the outside of the missile they are about to launch. One of the men reaches out his hand and wipes his finger along the small beads of liquid. He then holds it up to his nose, smells it, then tastes it.

"Wow," he croaks. "This stuff is great!"

His friend tries it and is amazed. "This stuff packs quite a punch!" he says.

So the two men wipe the condensation off with a towel and wring the towel out into a bucket. They then retire to the back of a toolshed to consume the remainder of their "discovery."

A couple of hours later one of the scientists receives a call from the other. He is surprised because it sounds like his friend is calling him long distance.

"It sounds like you are far away," says the man. "Where are you?"

"I'm in San Diego," says the other man.

"How did you get there so fast?" exclaims the first scientist.

"Remember that stuff we drank a couple of hours ago?" says the man in San Diego. "Well, let me give you a little advice: Don't fart."

* * *

Q: What's the difference between erotic and kinky?
A: Erotic, you use a feather—kinky, you use the whole chicken.

* * *

Three men—an American, an Englishman, and a Polish man— are being sent out on a survival test in the desert. They are asked what one thing it is that they want to take with them.

The American says, "I want to take some water so if I get thirsty, I have something to drink."

The Englishman says, "I want to take some food so if I get hungry, I will have something to eat."

The Polish man says, "I want to take a car door so if I get too hot, I can roll down the window."

*   *   *

A woman got into my cab one night and asked me how business was. I said, "It's been pretty slow."

She said, "Yeah, it's been pretty slow for me too."

"Oh, yeah?" I said. "What kind of work do you do?"

"Well," she said, "we're sort of in the same business. You drive around looking for a fare and I stand around waiting for one."

*   *   *

God is making all the creatures for the Earth and is giving out sex lives to each animal. First he turns to the human.

"I'm giving you ten years of a good sex life," says God.

The man's face falls. "Is that all?" he asks.

"I only have so much to go around, fella," says God. He then turns to the monkey and says, "I'm giving you twenty years of a good sex life."

The monkey says, "Oh, I don't really need that much. Ten years would be more than enough for me."

The man, standing nearby, overhears this and says excitedly, "*I'll* take it! I'll take those extra ten years!"

"All right," says God. "You got it." He then turns to the lion. 'I'm going to give you twenty years of a good sex life."

The lion replies, "You know, God, I really think I would be happier with just ten."

The man starts hopping up and down. "I'll take them! I'll take the other ten years!"

"You can have them," says God to the man. He then turns to the donkey and says, "Now I am going to give you twenty years of a good sex life. Is that all right with you?"

"To tell you the truth," says the donkey, "I would also be satisfied with just ten."

God looks over at the man, who begins pleading with Him. "Oh, please! Please let me have those extra ten years too!"

God gives the man the other ten years and then retires for the day.

This story explains why a man has ten years of a good sex life, ten years monekying around, ten years of lyin' about it, and then ten years of making an ass out of himself.

*　　*　　*

An old bull and a young bull are standing on top of a hill. At the foot of the hill is a large herd of heifers. The young bull turns to the old bull and says, "What do you say we run down the hill and screw a couple of those cows?"

The old bull replies, "What do you say we walk down and screw them all?"

*　　*　　*

Two women are in the kitchen preparing vegetables on a Friday night when one of the women looks out the window. She sees her husband coming up the walkway with a bouquet of flowers.

The wife turns to her friend and says, "Oh, darn! He's bringing flowers. That means another weekend on my back with my legs up in the air."

Her friend says, "What's the matter? Don't you have a vase?"

*　　*　　*

176

Q: What do you do if a Polish man throws a hand grenade at you?
A: Pull out the pin and throw it back.

* * *

The pope decides to visit America. When his plane arrives at JFK airport, a big crowd is there to meet him. As the pope steps off the plane the crowd chants, "Elvis! Elvis! Elvis!" and he says to them, "Oh, my children, thank you so much! But I am not Elvis."

He is picked up in a long white limousine that has "Elvis" written on the side in big, sparkling letters. As the pope steps into the limo he says, "Bless you, but I'm not Elvis."

The limo takes him to the Plaza Hotel where there is a huge crowd standing behind the police barricades. The people are shouting, "Elvis! Elvis! Elvis!"

He is taken up to his room, the largest suite in the hotel. As the pope begins to unpack his bags, the door to the adjoining room suddenly opens. In walk three beautiful women dressed in scanty negligees.

The pope looks at them for a moment, then sings, "Well, it's one for the money, two for the show . . ."

* * *

Two women from out of town got into my cab one afternoon during rush hour. They were going from Soho to Bloomingdales, quite a long trip at that time of day. After thirty-five minutes one of them suddenly turned to me and said excitedly, "We're getting close, aren't we?"

"Yes," I said. "We're at Fifty-eighth and Park, two blocks away."

"I knew it!" she proudly exclaimed. "My shopping nose could tell!"

* * *

A man and a woman get married, and on their wedding night, the man says to his wife, "Darling, I want you to give me a blow job."

"Absolutely not," says the woman. "If I did that, you wouldn't respect me in the morning."

"What do you mean?" says the man. "We went out with each other for ten years before we even got married. Of course I'll respect you."

"I won't do it," she says. "You won't respect me in the morning."

Ten years later, on their tenth wedding anniversary, the wife asks her husband, "What do you want for your anniversary this year?"

"You know," says the man, "we've been married ten years. I love you a lot, and really, all I want is for you to go down on me."

"I won't do that," says the woman. "You won't respect me in the morning."

"I won't respect you in the morning? After ten years of loyal matrimony?" says the man. "Don't be silly. Of course I'll respect you in the morning."

"I won't do it," she says.

On their fiftieth wedding anniversary their children throw a big party for them. After the big bash, when they get home, the wife says to her husband, "What do you want for your golden wedding anniversary?"

"I really just want one thing. I want you to give me a blow job," he says.

"I can't," she says once again. "You won't respect me in the morning."

"What do you mean?" says the man. "We're seventy years old and we've been married for fifty years! *Of course* I'll respect you in the morning."

She thinks for a moment, then says, "Well...it *has* been fifty years...."

"That's right!" he says. "We've been together *fifty years*! I respect you more than anyone on earth!"

"Well..." she says, "it *is* our fiftieth anniversary."

"That's right!" he says, "and I've never even *looked* at anyone else, and I'll respect you even *more* in the morning."

"You never did ask for much," she says.

"That's all I ever wanted," he says.

"Promise you'll respect me in the morning?" she asks.

"I promise!" he says.

So she finally decides that she will indeed give him a blow job. Just as she begins to do it, the telephone rings. The man leans over and answers it.

"Yes?" he says into the phone. "Yes, just a minute." He holds the receiver out to his wife and says, "It's for you, cocksucker."

* * *

Q: Did you hear about the Polish lottery?
A: If you win, you get a dollar a year for a million years.

* * *

Jesus is out on the golf course playing a few holes with St. Peter as his caddy. As he's about to make a drive Jesus turns to St. Peter and asks, "Which club do you think I should use for this shot?"

St. Peter looks over the course and says, "The seven iron."

"I don't know," says Jesus. "I think Arnold Palmer would use the nine."

St. Peter shakes his head. "I think you'd better use the seven iron, Jesus. Look, you have the sand trap in front of the green, and the lake beyond."

"Nah," says Jesus. "I think Arnold Palmer would use the nine. Give me the nine."

So St. Peter hands Jesus the nine iron, and Jesus hits the ball. It goes sailing out, bounces once on the green, and then splashes into the lake.

They go walking down to the lake, and, of course, Jesus walks across the water to fetch his ball.

A fellow happens to pass by, sees Jesus walking on the water, and says to St. Peter, "Who does that guy think he is, Jesus Christ?"

"Naaah," says St. Peter. "He thinks he's Arnold Palmer."

* * *

Q. What do you call a Norwegian car?
A. A Fjord.

* * *

A man goes into a bar, walks up to the bartender, and says, "I'll bet you fifty dollars that I can bite my eye."

"All right," says the bartender, and throws his fifty dollars down on the bar.

The man proceeds to take out a glass eye and then bites it. As the man pockets the money he looks at the bartender, who has suddenly become very depressed.

"I'll tell you what," says the man. "I'll give you a chance to make your money back. I'll bet you double or nothing that I can bite my other eye."

The bartender thinks to himself. "Well, he can't have *two* glass eyes," and throws another fifty dollars on the bar.

The man then takes out his false teeth and uses them to bite his other eye. So the bartender begins to sink into a real gloom, until the man says to him, "Okay, I'll make you one more bet. I'll bet you this hundred dollars to five of your dollars that you can slide a shot glass down the length of this bar, and I can run alongside it and piss into it without spilling a single drop."

The bartender thinks, "Well, what have I got to lose," and says to the man, "Okay the bet is on," and he fully expects the man once again to have a trick up his sleeve.

So he slides the shot glass down the bar, and the man runs alongside, trying to piss into the glass. But rather than getting it in the glass, he misses completely and the urine splashes all over the bar.

The bartender is so happy to have won his money back that he throws his hands over his head and starts jumping up and down, laughing and cheering. Just then a man at a table over in the corner of the room slams his fist down on his table and begins cursing loudly.

"Gee," says the bartender, "I wonder what's the matter with *him*?"

"Oh, him?" says the man, handing the bartender the hundred dollars. "I bet *him* a *thousand dollars* I could piss all over the bar and make the bartender happy about it."

* * *

A bum is walking along in the theater district just around matinee time. The streets are crowded with people rushing to get to their shows. The bum sees a well-dressed man walking along and goes up to him and asks, "Sir, can I borrow a quarter?"

The man stops and says in a very dignified tone, " 'Neither a borrower nor a lender be!'—William Shakespeare."

The bum looks back at him and says, " 'Up your asshole, you cocksucker!'—David Mamet."

*   *   *

Q: What do a woman in tight jeans and Brooklyn have in common?
A: Flatbush.

*   *   *

A couple is driving in the country. They have never had sex before because they are waiting until after they are married. This night it happens to be raining really hard and the roads become dangerous, so they stop at a motel.

"We would like two rooms," the man says.

"I'm sorry, sir," answers the desk clerk, "but we have only one room available. But it does have two twin beds."

The couple look at each other and shrug. "O.K.," says the man. "We'll take the room."

So they go in and he goes to his bed and she goes to hers. They turn out the lights and the woman says, "Honey, would you do me a favor, and please get me another blanket?"

The man says, "I have a better idea. Why don't we pretend we're married for fifteen minutes?"

She thinks for a moment and says, "Hmm...O.K."

So he says, "Get up and get your own 'damn' blanket!"

* * *

Q: How do you say "fuck you" in Yiddish?
A: "Trust me."

* * *

A man has a bad problem. His eyes bulge out. He is terribly embarrassed by it and has gone to doctor after doctor, but no one seems to be able to help him. Finally, in desperation, he looks in the Yellow Pages under "Eyes Bulging Doctors," and darned if there isn't one listing there. So he calls and makes an appointment.

He goes down to the office, and when he arrives, he is the only person in the waiting room. He begins to feel a little nervous about this, but then he thinks, "Well, this *is* a rare condition, and this doctor *is* a specialist." Finally he is admitted by the physician.

After examining him the doctor says, "Well, there *is* a cure for this condition but only one. I must cut your balls off."

The man's eyes bulge out even more, and as he's backing out the door, he says, "Thanks, Doc, but the problem isn't *that* bad."

He then goes home, and after a couple of weeks of thinking about it, he says to himself, "Well, I'm certainly not getting any girls with my eyes looking like this, so I might as well have the operation."

He returns to the doctor and says, "Okay, Doc, I can't stand it anymore. Do your dirtiest." So the doctor performs the castration, and sure enough the guy's eyes sink back into his head and he looks not only normal but actually quite attractive. He thanks the doctor profusely and is overjoyed.

In keeping with his new image he decides to buy himself a new suit. He goes to a tailor and says to him, "I'd like a navy blue pin-striped suit. No cuffs on the trousers and a medium-width lapel."

The tailor says, "Okay, come back in a week."

The guy says, "Gee, aren't you going to *measure* me or anything?"

"Nah," says the tailor. "I can just look at you and tell what size you are."

"But that's impossible," says the man.

"You wear a size forty-two jacket, right?"

"Wow! That's right!"

"And you have a thirty-two-inch inseam, right?"

"Wow! That's amazing!"

"And you have a thirty-six-inch waist, right?"

"Yes," says the guy.

"And you wear size forty underwear, right?"

"Now there you're wrong," the guy says to the tailor. "I wear size thirty-four underwear."

"No," says the tailor. "I've been in the business twenty years, I know what I'm talking about. You wear size forty underwear."

"No, I don't," says the guy. "I wear size thirty-four underwear."

"You *can't* wear size thirty-four underwear," says the tailor. "If you did, your *eyes* would bulge out!"

* * *

You know, sometimes you can learn a lot from what is written on bathroom walls. One day, in the men's room at the garage, I looked up and saw this scrawled on the wall:

Q: Do you know why dogs lick their balls?
A: Because they *can.*

* * *

A man is driving to work when he suddenly realizes that he has forgotten his wallet. He turns around and drives home to retrieve it. He goes upstairs and into his bedroom and sees his wife standing naked with her back to him, taking some money out of his wallet.

He sneaks up behind her and pats her on the bottom, saying, "How much today, honey?"

Without turning around the wife says, "Oh, the usual. Two quarts of milk and a dozen eggs."

* * *

During World War II an American is captured by the Germans in the African Desert. The man is brought before the Nazi commander and made to stand at attention under the blazing sun.

The commander says to the American, "We do not go by the usual laws and conventions out here in the desert. What we are going to do is give you a choice. We can execute you now, or you can try to pass three tests. If you pass all three tests, you may go free."

So the American says, "Well, what are the three tests?"

The German says, "You see those three tents over there? In the first tent are five bottles of vodka. You must go into that tent and drink all five bottles, until they are completely empty.

"Then you must go into the next tent. In that tent there is a lion with an impacted tooth. You must remove that impacted tooth from the lion's mouth with your bare hands.''

The American gulps, then asks, "What's in the third tent?''

"Should you pass the first two tests,'' says the Nazi commander, "in the third tent there is a woman who has never been sexually satisfied in her life. You must satisfy her totally and completely. She must walk out of the tent with you and say, 'I have been sexually satisfied beyond by wildest dreams.'

"After you have successfully completed those three tests you may go free.''

The American says to the commander, "The only other choice I have is execution, right?''

"That's right,'' says the German.

So the American goes into the first tent and drinks all five bottles of vodka. He then staggers out and asks to be pointed toward the second tent. The German soldiers push him in the right direction, and after much lurching and zigzagging, he enters the second tent.

All of a sudden the lion lets out a tremendous roar, and the walls of the tent begin to flap violently. This continues for quite a while with much roaring and crashing coming from inside the tent. Then suddenly everything is quiet and still. A few moments later the American soldier staggers out from the tent all bloody and scratched, his uniform in tatters.

He weaves up to the Nazi commander and says drunkenly, "All right now! Where's that bitch with the impacted tooth?''

* * *

Q: What is the last thing that goes through a mosquito's brain as he hits your windshield at sixty miles an hour?

A: His asshole.

* * *

A priest, a minister, and a rabbi are talking to one another. They begin discussing the monies their respective organizations take in and how they divide these monies up.

The priest says, "Well, after the collection I draw a line on the floor. Then I throw the money up in the air. Whatever lands on the right side is God's and whatever lands on the left side is mine."

The minister says, "Yes, I use a similar method. I draw a circle on the floor, then throw the money up in the air. Whatever lands inside the circle is God's and whatever lands outside I keep."

They both turn to the rabbi. "How do *you* do it?" asks the priest.

"Well," says the rabbi. "I use a similar method. I throw the money up in the air, and whatever God wants he keeps."

* * *

Q: How do you catch a unique rabbit?
A: Unique up on it.

Q: How do you catch a tame rabbit?
A: Tame way, unique up on it.

* * *

A man is calling on his best friend to pay a condolence call the day after the friend's wife has died. When he knocks on the door, he gets no answer, so he decides to go in and see if everything is all right. Upon entering the house, the man discovers his friend in the living room having sex with the maid.

"Jack!" says the man. "Your wife just died *yesterday*!"

His friend looks up and says, "In this grief do you think I know what I'm doing?"

*　　*　　*

Q: What did the elephant say to the nude man?
A: "How do you *breathe* through that thing?"

*　　*　　*

A man goes into a tavern and sees a gorilla standing behind the bar next to the bartender. "Hey, what's that gorilla doing there?" asks the man.

"He does tricks," says the bartender. "Take a look at this," he says, and picks up a baseball bat. He then rears back and whacks the gorilla across the forehead. The gorilla drops to his knees and gives the bartender a blow job.

When the gorilla is finished, the man says to the bartender, "That is the most amazing thing I've ever seen!"

"Would you care to give it a try?" asks the bartender.

"Well," says the man, a little hesitant, "okay, just don't hit me so hard."

*　　*　　*

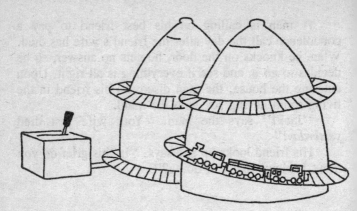

Q: What do electric train sets and women's breasts have in common?

A: They were both originally intended for children, but it's the fathers who play with them.

* * *

A Southern boy graduates from high school and is going north to college. Just as he is about to leave his parents say to him, "We know you're going to be mighty lonely up there with all them Northerners, so we decided to let you take Old Blue with you. He has been our family dog for so many years, we know that Old Blue will be good company for you."

So the boy goes north with Old Blue and is only there a few weeks when he gets a call from Mary Lou, his girlfriend back home. It seems that in about eight more months they will be having a problem unless she can take care of it now, and it will cost five hundred dollars.

The boy tells Mary Lou that he will get back to her. Then he calls his folks.

"How are you?" they ask.

"Oh, I'm just fine," he says.

"And how," they ask, "is Old Blue?"

"Well, he's kind of depressed. You see, there's this woman up here who's been teaching dogs to read, and Old Blue is feeling kind of left out 'cause all the dogs can read, exceptin' him. The woman charges five hundred dollars."

"Well," say the parents, "we won't let Old Blue down. We'll send you the money."

When the boy receives the five hundred dollars a few days later, he sends it off to Mary Lou and everything is taken care of.

The boy goes home for a quick visit, and a little over a month after he gets back to school, he receives another call from Mary Lou. It seems they have the same problem again and she needs another five hundred dollars.

So the boy calls his parents and tells them that while he, himself, is fine, Old Blue is depressed again. "Old Blue has been readin' up a storm," he tells them. "He's been through all the books in the library and is now reading all the newspapers and magazines. But now the lady is teaching the dogs to talk, and Old Blue is feeling left out again. She charges five hundred dollars for talking lessons."

"We can't let Old Blue down," say the parents. "We'll send you the money."

Once again, the boy gets the money and sends it off to Mary Lou.

Then the boy is driving home in his pickup for Christmas vacation with Old Blue sitting on the seat next to him, and he just can't figure out what he is going to tell his parents. When he's in front of the Bufords' farm, the farm next to his parents', he takes his shotgun and Old Blue out of the car and shoots the dog, killing him.

When the boy reaches his parents' farm, he sees his father standing out in the driveway.

"Hello, son!" says the father. He then looks at the pickup and asks, "But where's Old Blue?"

"Well, Pa," says the boy, "I was driving down the road and Old Blue was reading Shakespeare and Plato and pontificating on Newton and Socrates when we passed the Bufords' farm. Old Blue said to me, 'Say, what do you think your mother would do if I told her that your father has been running over to the Bufords' farm and screwing Mrs. Buford all these years?'"

The father looks at his son and says, "You shot that dog, didn't you, boy?"

*　　*　　*

An eighty-year-old man marries a twenty-year-old girl. A friend says to him, "Hey, can't that be fatal?"

The old man says, "If she *dies*, she *dies*."

*　　*　　*

As I mentioned before, the Brazilians have Portuguese jokes. A Brazilian man once told me that the only thing in Brazil considered dumber than a Portuguese man is a Brazilian president. He then told me this joke:

A Portuguese man has an appointment to see the

Brazilian president. He arrives two hours late, and the president is furious.

"Where were you?" says the president. "I've been waiting two hours!"

"I know, I'm sorry," says the man. "But I was riding up an escalator when it broke down. And do you know, I had to stand there for *two hours* while they fixed it!"

The Brazilian president throws up his hands in exasperation. "You idiot!" he yells. "Do you mean to tell me that you were *standing* on the escalator for *two hours* before they got it fixed?"

"Yes," says the Portuguese man.

"You stupid jerk!" says the president. "Why didn't you *sit down*?"

* * *

Q: What do Thom McAnn's and the post office have in common?
A: 25,000 loafers.

* * *

Three men die and go to heaven. At the gate St. Peter tells them, "Before you go into heaven, we are going to give you each a vehicle with which to get around. The way we determine what type of vehicle you will get is by how faithful you were to your wives. Now," he says, turning to the first man, "were you true to your wife?"

"Yes, I was, St. Peter," says the first man. "I never strayed. From the day I married her to the day I died, I slept with no woman other than my wife. I loved her very deeply."

"As reward for your complete fidelity," says St. Peter, "I now give you these keys to a beautiful Rolls-Royce."

The man happily accepts the keys, and St. Peter turns to the second man. "Sir," he says, "were you faithful to your wife?"

"Well, St. Peter," says the second man a little shyly, "I must admit that when I was much younger, I did stray once or twice. But I did love my wife very much, and after those minor indiscretions, I was completely faithful until my dying day."

St. Peter looks down at the man and says, "As a reward for good marital conduct, I am giving you these keys to a Pontiac."

As the man takes the keys from him St. Peter turns to the third man. "Sir," he says, "were you faithful to your wife?"

"St. Peter," says the man, "I screwed everything I could, every chance I got. There wasn't a week of my marriage that I didn't sleep with someone other than my wife. But I must admit to you, St. Peter, that it was a problem I had, because I really did love my wife very much."

"Well," says St. Peter, "we do know that you did love you wife and that *does* count for something, so this is what you get." With that he rolls out a ten-speed bicycle and gives it to the man. The gates of heaven open, and the three men enter.

Sometime later the man on the bicycle is riding along, when he sees that the man with the Rolls-Royce has pulled over and is sitting on the bumper of his car. He is sobbing uncontrollably. The man pulls his bicycle up next to the man and says, "Hey, pal, what's the matter? What could possibly be wrong? You have a beautiful Rolls-Royce to drive around in."

"I know," says the man through his sobs, "but I just saw my wife on roller skates!"

* * *

Q: What do you call a Polish man with a five hundred dollar hat?

A: Pope.

* * *

A man is talking to his best friend about married life. "You know," he says, "I really trust my wife, and I think she has always been faithful to me, but you know, there's *always* that doubt. There's *always* that doubt."

His friend says, "Yeah, I know what you mean."

A couple of weeks later the man has to go out of town on business. Before he goes, he gets together with his friend.

"Pal," he says, "while I'm away, could you do me a favor? Could you watch my house and see if there is anything fishy going on? I mean, I trust my wife, but . . . there's *always* that doubt. There's *always* that doubt."

The friend agrees to help out, and the man leaves town. Two weeks later he comes back and meets up with his buddy. "So," he says, "did anything happen?"

"I have some bad news for you," says the friend. "The day after you left I saw a strange car pull up in front of your house. The horn honked, and your wife ran out and got into the car, then they drove off. Later, after dark, the car came back, and I saw your wife and a strange man get out. They went into the house and I saw the upstairs light go on, so I ran over and looked in the window. I saw your wife kissing the man. Then he took off his shirt. Then she took off her blouse. Then they turned out the light.

"*Then* what happened?" says the man, his eyes opening wide.

"I don't know," says the friend. "It was too dark for me to see."

"Damn," says the man. "You see what I mean? There's *always* that doubt. There's *always* that doubt."

*　　*　　*

Did you hear about the man who made a fortune by going over to Poland with a hundred cases of Cheerios and selling them as bagel seeds?

*　　*　　*

Four nuns die in a car crash. They are standing before the pearly gates with St. Peter. St. Peter says to the first one, "Sister, have you ever sinned?"

The first nun replies, "I kissed a man once."

St. Peter says to her, "Go wash you lips in the holy water and go on into heaven."

After the nun does this the gates open and in she goes.

St. Peter asks the next nun, "Sister, have you ever sinned?"

"St. Peter," says the second nun, "I once touched a man's penis."

"Well, then," replies St. Peter, "wash your hand in the holy water and enter into heaven."

The nun does as she is told and then walks in through the gates.

As St. Peter turns to ask the next nun he sees the

last two of them pushing and shoving, jostling for position.

"Hey, hey," he says, "what's going on here?"

"Well," says one of the nuns, "is it all right if I gargle with that before she sits in it?"

* * *

Q: What's the difference between a rock musician and a pig?

A: A pig wouldn't stay up all night screwing a rock musician.

* * *

A man goes in to see the doctor. "Doc," he says, "I can't shit."

The doctor says, "I'll give you a prescription for some pills. Take one every four hours and this should take care of the problem. If for some reason the trouble persists for longer than a week, come back and see me again."

The following week the man is back in the doctor's office. "Doc," he says, "I still can't shit."

"All right," says the doctor. "I'm going to prescribe some more pills for you. These are a bit stronger than the last ones and you should take *two*, every *three* hours. This should definately clear up the problem, but once again, if you're still having any difficulty in another week, come back to see me."

A week goes by, and once again the man shows up at the doctor's office. "Doc," he says, "I'm freaking out. I *still* can't shit."

"Have you been taking the pills as I prescribed?" asks the doctor. When the man says that he has, the doctor gets out his pad and pencil. "Hmmm. This *does* sound rather serious," he says. "I had better get some more information about you. Now, I have you name, what's your address?" The man tells him. "And what," asks the doctor, "is your occupation?"

The man says, "I am a musician."

"A musician?" says the doctor. "A musician? Why didn't you tell me you were a musician in the first place? Here," he says as he reaches for his wallet, "let me give you some money so you can buy some *food*."

*　　*　　*

Q: A man is trying to decide among three women, which one he will marry. He gives them each $1,000. The first one spends $800 on clothes and puts the other $200 in the bank. The second one spends $200 on clothes and puts the other $800 in the bank. The third one puts the whole $1,000 in the bank. Which one did the man marry?

A: The one with the big tits.

*　　*　　*

202

Q: Why couldn't the Polish terrorist blow up a bus?
A: He kept burning his lips on the tailpipe.

* * *

Superman has always had a big crush on Wonder Woman. One day, while flying over Metropolis, he looks down and happens to see Wonder Woman lying on her back, spread-eagled on top of a building, totally naked.

Without a moment's hesitation he flys down, lands on the roof, throws off his cape and his clothes, and then jumps on her. He goes at it quite a while, and when he is finished, he rolls off her and says, "Wow! Thank you! That was the best I've ever had in my entire life!"

"Well, you're welcome!" says Wonder Woman. "I just wonder if the Invisible Man will ever walk again."

* * *

On the first day of school a teacher is introducing herself to her new third-grade class. "Children," she says, "My name is Miss Prussy. Now I'll write it on the blackboard for you." As she does this, she says, "An easy way to remember my name is that it is spelled just like 'pussy' but with an 'r'."

The following day she asks her class, "Boys and girls, can any of you remember my name?"

"I know," says one boy eagerly. "It's Miss Crunt!"

* * *

A guy is walking around his neighborhood looking for odd jobs but with no luck. Finally a man feels sorry for the guy and decides to give him a job.

He calls the guy down into his basement and says, "Have you ever done any painting before?"

"A little," says the guy.

"All right," says the man. "This isn't too difficult a job. What I want you to do is paint my porch. I've already bought the green paint and the brushes. Everything else you will need is out in the garage. I'll be working down here in the basement if you have any questions."

A few hours later the guy knocks on the basement door. When the man answers, the guy, splattered all over with green paint, tells him, "I'm finished."

"Already?" says the man. "That was quick."

"Yessiree," says the guy. "But I must say, it sure looked more like a Ferrari to me."

*　　*　　*

An old woman wakes up one morning to find that the nearby river has overflowed and flooded her entire house. She cannot even go downstairs because the water has risen above the first floor. As she leans out her second-story window she sees that the water is still rising.

Just then, a man in a rowboat happens to pass by. The man yells to her, "C'mon lady! Jump in! I'll save you!"

"No, thank you," says the woman, "the *Lord* will provide."

"All right, lady," says the man, "suit yourself," and he rows on.

The water rises, and the old woman must leave her second story and climb out onto the roof. She is sitting on her roof when a small motorboat with two men in it passes by.

"Come on, lady!" yells a man in the boat. "Jump in! We'll save you!"

"No, thank you," answers the woman. "The *Lord* will provide."

The boat motors on, and the waters rise. The woman climbs up onto her chimney, the only part of her house that is not completely submerged. A big motor launch comes by and stops near her. "Jump in, lady! Come on! We'll save you!"

"No, thank you," says the old woman. "The *Lord* will provide."

The boat drives away, and soon the water rises above the chimney and the woman drowns.

As she arrives in heaven the rather annoyed woman demands to see God. When she is brought before him, she says, "Hey! What happened? I thought the *Lord* would *provide*!"

"For cryin' out loud, lady," says God, "I *sent three boats*!"

*   *   *

Q: What do you get when you cross a Cabbage Patch doll with the Pillsbury doughboy?
A: A rich bitch with a yeast infection.

*   *   *

A man goes to the doctor, and the doctor tells him that he only has twelve hours to live. So he goes home and tells his wife, and she cries and cries. Then she holds him and announces, "I'm going to make this the best night of your life."

He says, "It's the last."

And she says, "But it'll be the *best*!" So she lights candles, makes his favorite dinner, and opens a bottle of their favorite champagne.

They have a wonderful dinner and then go straight to bed. They make love, and just as they're about to fall asleep, he taps her on the shoulder and says, "Honey, could we do it again?"

So they make love again, and just as she's about to fall asleep, he taps her on the shoulder, saying "Sweetheart, could we do that once again?"

So they do it again, and just as she's about to fall asleep, he taps her on the shoulder and says, "Darling, could we please just do that one more time?"

The woman replies, "Sure! What do *you* care? *You* don't have to get up in the morning."

* * *

Q: What is the Jewish dilemma?
A: Pork chops at half price.

* * *

St. Peter has to go to the bathroom. He has been standing guard at the pearly gates for five hundred years, and he really has to go. He asks Jesus, "Hey, look, can you do me a favor? Take over here for a few minutes while I go to the bathroom."

Jesus says, "But I've never done this before."

"It's nothing," says St. Peter. "Here's a pad and a pencil. When people come up, you ask them their name, where they lived, get their occupation, and ask them any pertinent questions. If they sound cool, let them in. That's all there is to it. I've gotta go." And he runs off.

A few minutes later an old man comes up, and Jesus asks him, "What's your name?"

The little old man says, "In English I think you would say my name is Joseph."

"And what," says Jesus, "was your occupation?"

"I was a carpenter," says Joseph.

"Okay," says Jesus, writing all this down. He looks carefully at the man, then asks, "Did you have any children?"

"Yes," says the man. "I had a son."

Jesus looks at these three answers. Then looks back at the man. He then asks, "Was there anything unusual about your son?"

"Yes," says the old man. "My son did not come into this world in the usual way. He also had nail holes in his hands and his feet—"

At which point Jesus throws open his arms and says, "Dad!"

The old man looks up at Jesus and says, "Pinocchio?"

*   *   *

A woman got into my cab one night. I tried telling her a few jokes, but she wasn't very responsive. After telling her one of my best ones and getting dead silence, I just said, "Okay, I'll shut up."

She apologized for not laughing and said, "You see I hardly ever laugh out loud. There is only one joke that has ever made me really laugh, and I heard that a few months ago.

"The problem," she went on, "is that I can't

remember this joke. It has been driving me crazy. I can remember how it starts, but I haven't been able to find anyone who knows the ending. I have been searching for months.''

Knowing the extensive catalog of jokes in my head, I said to her, "Well, why don't you start telling it to me? Maybe I can fill in the ending for you.''

"Well . . . okay,'' she said, somewhat skeptically, and then began:

A woman goes into an ice cream parlor. She walks up to the man behind the counter and says, "I want some chocolate ice cream, please.''

"I'm sorry, madam,'' says the man, "but I'm afraid we're out of chocolate.''

"Oh,'' says the woman. "In that case I'll take some chocolate.''

At this point I said, "Oh, yeah! I know that joke!'' And I took it from there:

So the man says, "No, no, madam. You don't understand. We have *run out* of chocolate.''

"Oh,'' replies the woman. "Well, then, I'll just have chocolate.''

The man behind the counter looks at the woman and says, "Okay, spell 'van,' as in 'vanilla.' ''

At this point the woman in the backseat got very excited. "That's it! she said. "That's the joke!'' So I went on:

So the woman spells "V-a-n.''

"All right,'' says the man behind the counter, "spell 'straw,' as in 'strawberry.' ''

The woman says, "Okay. S-t-r-a-w.''

"Good!" says the man. "Now spell 'fuck,' as in chocolate."

The woman looks at the man and says, "But there's no 'fuck' in chocolate."

The man shouts, *"That's what I've been trying to tell you!"*

I couldn't have timed it better. Just as I hit the punch line we arrived at the woman's destination. "Thank you so much!" said the woman. "I'm giving you a big tip, because it was really worth it. Now I feel like I can let out a huge sigh of relief."

It was one of those moments that makes driving a cab seem worthwhile.

* * *

Q: What do a walrus and Tupperware have in common?
A: They both work well with tight seals.

* * *

A worm comes up from a hole in the ground and sees another worm sticking out of a hole in the ground nearby. The worm says, "Hey, cutie, how about a date?"

The other worm says, "What are you talking about? I'm your other end!"

(Author's note: *I must confess that this joke is not one I heard from a passenger. My father has been trying to get this into the book since the day he heard about my contract, so this one is from, and for, him.*)

* * *

Q: What's the difference between mashed potatoes and pea soup?

A: Anyone can mash potatoes.

* * *

A newlywed couple has just undressed and gotten into bed when the wife says to the husband, "Sweetheart, could you please get me that jar of Vaseline from the top left-hand drawer of the bureau?"

"Honey," says the man, "you won't need any Vaseline."

"Yes, I will, dear," she says. "Please get it for me."

"All right, lover," says the husband, and he gets out of the bed. When he gives her the Vaseline, she takes it all out of the jar and smears it all over her crotch area.

Upon seeing this the husband says, "Dear, you know that long string of pearls I gave you? Could you please get them for me out of the top right-hand drawer of the bureau?"

"Of course," says the woman. She goes and gets the pearls and hands them to the man. After he puts them on she says to him. "Why darling, what on earth are you doing?"

"Well," says the husband, looking down at the Vaseline smeared all over her, "if you think I'm going into a mess like that without chains, you're crazy!"

* * *

A little boy gets up to go to the bathroom in the middle of the night. As he passes his parents' bedroom he peeks in through the keyhold. He watches for a moment, then continues on down the hallway, saying to himself. *"Boy,* and she gets mad at *me* for sucking my *thumb."*

*   *   *

A man visiting the president in the Oval Office is very curious about all the different telephones on his desk. When asked what each one is for, the president gladly explains.

"You see this red one here?" he says to the man. "This connects me directly to the premier in Moscow. And this white one here is my direct line to God."

"Wow!" says the man. "A direct line to God! Tell me, how much would a call to God cost?"

"Oh," says the president, "it's about a thousand dollars a minute."

When the man leaves the president, he is very impressed.

A couple of months later he happens to visit the prime minister of Israel in the leader's office. Once again he is struck with the number of telephones on the man's desk.

"Ah, yes," says the prime minister, explaining his setup. "This blue phone is a direct line to the president of the United States, and this red phone is a direct line to the premier of the U.S.S.R. Do you know that it costs me two hundred dollars a minute to speak to the Russian premier?"

"That certainly is a lot of money," says the man, "but what is that white phone there?"

"Oh"—the prime minister smiles—"that is my direct line to God."

"And how much," asks the man, "does that cost you?"

"Twenty-five cents," replies the prime minister.

"Twenty-five cents!" says the man in astonishment. "When I visited the president of the United States, he told me it cost *him* a thousand dollars to talk to God!

"Well, you see," says the prime minister. "From *here* it's a local call."

*　　*　　*

A ventriloquist is driving out to the West Coast for an engagement, but when he reaches New Mexico, his car begins to make a strange noise. He pulls into a service station in the middle of the desert and has the mechanic check it out. The mechanic says that he can fix it, but it will take about an hour. So rather than take a chance on being stranded somewhere, the man tells the mechanic to go ahead and repair the car.

The ventriloquist goes out in front of the gas station and is wondering how he is going to kill an hour in the middle of the desert. Just then, an Indian rides up on horseback. Next to the horse runs a dog, and behind are a dozen sheep.

"Ah," says the man to himself. "I can spend a little time having some fun with this Indian."

So he walks up to the Indian and says, "Sir, this a mighty fine-looking horse. Do you mind if I ask him a few questions?"

The Indian eyes the man suspiciously and says, "*Horse* no talk."

The man goes around to the front of the horse and says, "How do you like living with this Indian?"

Then, in his best horse voice he makes the horse appear to answer, "Gee, it's great! He feeds me well. He doesn't work me too hard. He takes real good care of me. I like him a lot."

Now the Indian is in total shock. He can't believe that his horse has just been talking. The ventriloquist then asks the Indian, "Do you mind if I ask your dog a few questions?"

The Indian looks sternly at the man and says, "*Dog* no talk."

But the man walks up to the dog and says, "So, how do you like having this Indian for a master?"

"Oh," says the ventriloquist in his best dog voice, "he's really nice. He always gives me enough food. He takes me hunting with him. His squaw is really nice too."

The Indian is now completely dumfounded. He can't believe that the two animals he has had for years have suddenly begun talking.

Then the ventriloquist goes up to the Indian and says, "Look, I don't want to take any more of your time. But before you go, do you mind if I just ask your sheep one question?"

The Indian's eyes widen, and he says, "Sheep *lie*!"

*　　*　　*

Q: What do you call masturbating cows?
A: Beef strokin' off.

* * *

Two pirates are sitting in a tavern, talking. One of them has a hook instead of a hand, and an eye patch. The other pirate has a wooden leg. After a couple of pints of beer, they decide to tell each other how they got their injuries.

"One day," says the first pirate, "we had pulled alongside a merchant marine ship and were boarding her. I had my sword drawn when suddenly a man with a saber caught me by surprise and chopped my hand off. So I had this hook put on. How did you lose your leg?"

"There was a terrific storm at sea," begins the second pirate. "I was on deck when a gust of wind blew the mast over. It fell on my leg, pinning me to the deck. I would have drowned if they hadn't cut off my leg and freed me. So I had this wooden leg put on. Now, tell me, how did you lose your eye?"

"Uh, well," says the first pirate, fidgeting, "I don't really want to talk about it."

"Come on," says the second pirate, "we made a deal to tell each other about these things. What happened?"

"Well," says the first pirate, "a seagull shit in my eye."

"A seagull shit in your eye?" says the second pirate. "I can see how that would be uncomfortable and annoying, but it wouldn't cause you to *lose* the eye."

The first pirate replies, "But you see, it was my first day with the hook."

* * *

Your brother, your best friend, and you all die. You go to heaven, and as you enter the gates, an angel comes up and takes your brother by the hand. The angel leads him to a room, and there, standing in the room, is the ugliest woman he has ever seen. She is extremely fat, has greasy hair, and smells so bad, he can hardly stay in the room. The angel says to your brother, "As a reward for the way you spent your life, you must spend a hundred years with this woman."

The angel comes back out, takes your best friend by the hand and leads him to another room. There is the ugliest woman *he* has ever seen. She is just skin and bones with rotting teeth and warts all over her body. "As a reward for the way you spent your life," says the angel, "you must spend two hundred years with this woman."

The angel comes back out, takes you by the hand, and leads you to a room. Standing there is the most well-built, beautiful blond you've ever seen. The angel turns to the blond and says, "As a reward for the way you spent your life . . ."

* * *

Q: Why are there no ice cubes in Poland?
A: The old lady who had the recipe died.

* * *

A Polish man walks into a hardware store. He goes up to the owner standing at the cash register and asks for a job.

"Well," says the owner, "at the moment I *do* happen to need somebody. But tell me, can you *sell*?"

"Sure," says the man.

"I'm not sure if you really understand me," says the owner. "I mean, can you *sell*?"

"Yep," says the man, "I can."

The owner sees a customer coming in the door and says, "Okay, just to make sure you know what I'm talking about, watch me!"

The customer walks up and asks where the grass seed is. The owner tells him that it is in the third aisle over, the fourth shelf down. When the man comes back to the cash register with the grass seed, the owner says to him, "Do you need a lawn mower? We have a special sale on lawn mowers at the moment."

"What do I need a lawn mower for?" says the customer. "I don't even have any grass yet."

"Maybe not now," the owner replies, "but eventually you will. And then you'll need a lawn mower, and you won't be able to get one any cheaper than what we're selling them for now.

"Hmmm, I guess you're right," says the customer. Okay, I'll take the lawn mower too."

After the customer leaves the owner says to the Polish guy, "So, do you think you can do that?"

"Sure," he says.

"Okay," says the owner, "I have to make a deposit at the bank. I'll only be gone a few minutes, but while I'm away, watch over the store for me. And remember, if anyone comes in, *sell, sell, sell!*"

So the owner leaves, and a few minutes later a woman comes in. She goes up to the Polish man at the cash register and asks where the tampons are.

"Fifth aisle over, second shelf down," the man tells her.

When she comes back to pay for them, he asks her. "you wanna buy a lawn mower?"

"What would I want a lawn mower for?" she asks.

"Well," says the man, "you ain't gonna be fuckin', so you might as well mow the lawn."

* * *

A little Mexican boy comes home from school one day and says to his father, "Daddy, today we were studying history and the teacher told us about Pancho the bandit. Do you know Pancho the bandit?"

"Do *I* know Pancho the bandit?" asks the father. "Why, just a few years ago I was riding into town on my horse. Suddenly, from behind some bushes jumped Pancho the bandit with his six-guns drawn!

"He told me to get down off the horse and give him all my money. Pancho had the *guns,* so I got down off the horse and gave him all my money. Just then, my horse took a shit.

"Pancho told me to eat the shit. Pancho had the *guns,* so I ate the shit. Suddenly, my horse reared up and knocked the guns out of Pancho's hands and into the air. *I* caught the guns.

"I said to Pancho, 'Okay, now it's *your* turn. *You* eat the shit.' *I* had the guns, so Pancho ate the shit.

"And you ask me, son, if *I* know Pancho the bandit? Why, we had *lunch* together!"

* * *

A Polish carpenter is working on a building going up. He is on the second story using a chain saw when he accidentally slices off one of his ears. He looks down to the ground and, in hopes of finding his ear and

219

having it sewn back on, calls down to the men working below.

"Hey," he shouts, "do any of you guys see an ear down there?"

One of the men glances around, then yells up "Hey, buddy! Is this it?"

The Polish guy peers down, then calls out, "No. mine had a pencil behind it."

* * *

Q: Did you hear about the new Polish delicacy?
A: Pork tartare.

* * *

A man has an extremely large penis, but he also has a very bad stutter. Every time he meets a woman he begins to stutter so badly that he can't say anything to her.

Because of this problem he doesn't have any sex life at all. So he goes to a doctor, and gradually he manages to explain his problem to the doctor. The physician examines him and says, "Well, I see exactly what your problem is. The weight of your penis is pulling on your vocal cords and causing you to stutter. To cure your stuttering I must amputate ten inches from your penis."

The man has become so desperate, never even having had a date with a woman, that he agrees to the operation and has the ten inches amputated. Immediately his problem clears up. Without the stuttering he easily meets many women and they all love him and find him very charming. However, when they go to bed with him, they are all very, very disappointed.

After this goes on for a while he goes back to the doctor. "Doc," he says, "you were absolutely right. I want to thank you for curing my stuttering, but you know, I've really missed having that substantial penis. I now have decided that I want you to graft it back on."

The doctor says to him, "I'm s-s-sorry, but that's imp-p-possible."

* * *

Q: What's the difference between a Jewish mother and a vulture?
A: A vulture waits until you're dead to eat your heart out.

* * *

Two men are playing golf at a country club next to a cemetery. One of the men is just about to make an important putt when he looks up and sees a funeral procession going by. He stops, straightens up, takes off his golf cap, and holds it over his heart until the procession has gone by.

As he puts his hat back on his friend says to him, "That was a really nice, thoughtful gesture."

"Well," says the man as he bends down, returning to his putt, "after twenty years of marriage to her, it's the least I could do."

* * *

A man is showing his friend his bee collection when his friend says, "Hey, you had better poke some holes in the top of that jar, otherwise, the bees are going to die."

"Ah," says the man, "what do I care? It's only a hobby for me."

*　　*　　*

Two worms who live under a golf course wake up one morning. One says to the other, "Go up top and see if it's raining."

The other worm says, "I don't want to. If it *is* raining, I'll get all wet." So they argue back and forth like this until they decide to draw straws. One of them wins, and the other has to go up and check.

Just at this minute two women golfers happen to be passing overhead. One mentions that she has to pee, and the other woman says, "Hey, look. There is nobody else around. Why don't you do it right here?"

So the woman squats down and takes a piss at the exact moment the little worm breaks through the surface. He takes one look around, gets totally drenched, and hurries back down below.

The other worm says, "So, I see it's raining."

"Yeah," says the worm, wiping off his face. "As a matter of fact, it's raining so hard that the birds are building their nests upside down!"

*　　*　　*

Q: What was the snowman waiting for?
A: The snow blower.

*　　*　　*

A nun is living in a very strict convent where they are only allowed to say two words every ten years. After her first ten years the nun very carefully considers what two words she will say.

She thinks about it and thinks about it, until they bring her before the Mother Superior. She then says to the Mother Superior, very slowly, "Bed's hard."

Ten more years go by, and once again the nun must decide what two words best describe her feelings. When she is taken in to see the Mother Superior, she once again speaks very slowly and says, "Food bad."

After ten more years, thirty years in all that she has been living in the convent, the nun once again thoughtfully chooses her two words. Slowly and deliberately she says to the Mother Superior, "I quit."

The Mother Superior says, "I'm not surprised! For thirty years all you've done is *bitch, bitch, bitch.*"

* * *

One overhears some pretty strange conversations while driving a cab. One night I heard a man say to the woman next to him, "Tonight we're going to do every drug known to man."

"Okay," said the woman.

"You'll forget your problems," continued the man. "Everything will be wonderful, and if you're lucky," he said cheerfully, "you'll die!"

* * *

The Lone Ranger is about to be hung by rustlers who caught him spying on their camp. His only hope is Tonto, who managed to escape and go for help. As the bandits are putting the noose around the Lone Ranger's neck, he sees three horses approaching at a gallop. Sure enough, as they get closer he can see that it is Tonto on the first horse, but he can't make out who the other two riders are.

The Lone Ranger finally sees that Tonto is riding with two beautiful naked women. One is blond, and the other one brunette. The riders burst into the robbers' camp, and Tonto rides up to the Lone Ranger, saying, "Kemosabe, I have returned with the people you asked me to get."

"Tonto, you idiot," says the Lone Ranger, "I told you to go get *posse*!

*   *   *

Q: How do you get five pounds of meat out of a fly?
A: Unzip it.

*   *   *

A woman calls her butler into her bedroom, "Charles," she says.

"Yes, madam?" answers the butler.

"Charles, take off my dress."

"Yes, madam," he says, and removes the dress.

"Charles, take off my bra."

"Yes, madam," he says, and he takes off her bra.

"Now, Charles, take off my shoes and stockings."

"Yes, madam," he says as he removes her shoes and stockings.

"Now," says the woman, "take off my panties.

And I'm warning you, Charles: You're going to lose your job if I ever catch you wearing my clothes again."

* * *

An Englishman told me this Irish joke:

Q: Why do the Irish have potatoes and the Arabs have oil?

A: The Irish got first choice.

* * *

A drunk is sitting at a bar. He calls the bartender over, pointing to a woman sitting at the other end of the bar, and says to the bartender, "I wanna buy that douche bag a drink."

"Sir," says the bartender, "that happens to be a *lady*. Now, if you would care to refer to her as such, I will be glad to get her a drink for you."

The drunk says, "Okay, I wanna buy that douche bag a drink," and points again to the same woman.

"Sir," says the bartender, a bit more firmly, "if you cannot refer to the lady in the proper manner, I will not get her a drink for you."

Now by this time the drunk is beginning to get loud; "I wanna buy that douche bag a drink! I wanna buy that douche bag a drink."

The bartender, afraid that the lady will hear, says, "All right, buddy, all right. Just keep your voice down."

So he walks over to the lady and says, "Excuse me, ma'am, but that man over there wants to buy you a drink. What would you like?"

The woman smiles and says, "Vinegar and water."

Q: What did the hurricane say to the palm tree?

A: Hold on to your nuts, this isn't going to be just any old ordinary blow job!

* * *

An Irish Anglican minister arrives at Kennedy airport and, as luck would have it, gets a devout Irish Catholic cabdriver for his trip into the city. He tells the driver, "Take me to the Christ Church in Manhattan, please."

So the cabbie drives from the airport into Manhattan, goes straight up Fifth Avenue, and stops in front of St. Patrick's Cathedral. The minister is very angry and insulted and says to the driver, "Sir, I asked you to take me to the *Christ Church*!"

"Ah, Pastor, I know this town well. If He's home at all," says the cabbie, pointing to St. Patrick's, "He'll be in there."

* * *

A man gets sent to a small Midwestern town on business. He is going to be staying a few months, so after a couple of days he goes into the bar to try to make some friends. Something, however, has seemed strange to him about this town ever since he arrived, and after just a few minutes in the bar, he realizes what it is.

"Say," he says to the bartender, "aren't there any women in this town?"

"Nah," says the bartender, "the men here are all such jerks that the women just picked up and left."

"Gee," says the salesman, "that's terrible. But tell me, what do the men here do for dates and sex?"

"Oh, they do it with pigs," answers the bartender.

"Ugh!" says the man. "That is disgusting!"

Well, a couple of weeks goes by, and the man begins to feel the urge. He goes back into the bar and says to the bartender, "By the way, could you maybe tell me where the men in this town go to find the pigs they go out with?"

"Oh, sure!" says the bartender. "You just go up to the top of that hill and all the pigs are right there in the barnyard."

"Uh, thanks," says the salesman.

He walks up the hill and looks in the barnyard. One look at the pigs slopping around and he is so revolted that he almost leaves. But suddenly, over in the corner, he sees the cutest, plumpest little pig he has ever seen. She has big brown eyes, curly eyelashes, and a little curlicue with a bow on top of her head.

So he takes the pig out of the sty and back into town. He walks in through the doors of the bar, and when everyone sees him with the pig, there is quite a commotion, and they all move as far away from him as possible.

"Hey," says the man, going up to the bartender, "what's the matter with *them*? You told me *everyone* in this town goes out with pigs."

"Yeah, I know," says the bartender, "but I wasn't expecting you to take the *sheriff's* girl!"

* * *

On the most enjoyable trip to La Guardia Airport that I ever had, one of two very nice Midwestern women told me this joke:

Q: Why was the rubber flying through the air?
A: It got pissed off.

* * *

A man walks into a bar with a dog. The bouncer inside the door says, "Hey! You can't bring that dog in here!"

The man says, "Oh, you don't understand. This isn't a regular dog. This dog can talk."

"Oh, yeah?" The bouncer sneers. "A hundred bucks says he can't."

So the man says, "Okay, you're on," and turns to the dog.

"Okay, boy," he says, "tell me, what's on top of a house?"

The dog says, "Roof!"

"And what," says the man, "is on the outside of a tree?"

"Bark!" says the dog.

"Now," says the man, "who was the greatest baseball player who ever lived?"

"Ruth!" says the dog.

At this point the bouncer grabs the man by the collar and snarls, "Get outta here!" And he roughly throws him into the street.

The dog follows the man out, looks up at him, and says, "Gee. Do you think I should have said 'DiMaggio'?"

*   *   *

A man is standing up in front of the judge, asking for a divorce. The judge says to him, "All right, sir, please tell me why you want a divorce."

"Because," says the man, "I live in a two-story house."

"You live in a two-story house?" says the judge. "What kind of a reason is that for a divorce?"

"Well," says the man, "one story is, 'I've got a headache' and the other is, 'It's the wrong time of the month.'"

* * *

During the French Revolution a series of horrible murders was committed. The authorities were unable to determine exactly who the killer was, but they did manage to narrow it down to three suspects: A Frenchman, a German, and a Polish man. Given the heinous nature of the crimes, they decided to execute all three men, just to make sure that the killer would never kill again.

On the execution day all the people gathered in the town square. The three suspects were brought together on the platform next to the guillotine. It was decided that the Frenchman would be the first to die.

"How do you want to lie in the guillotine?" asked the executioner, "facedown or faceup?"

The Frenchman stepped forward with dignity and said, "Since I am going to meet my maker, I would like to face the heavens as I die. I will go faceup."

So they put the Frenchman in the guillotine faceup and released the blade. The blade slid smoothly down, until an inch above the Frenchman's neck, when it suddenly stopped.

"Free him! Free him!" cried everyone in the crowd. "The gods have spoken! He must be innocent!"

The executioner took the Frenchman out and let him go. Next he asked the German whether he wanted to go in the guillotine facedown or faceup.

"Since I have come from the earth and am going to return to the earth, I would like to face the ground as I die," said the German. "I will go facedown."

So they put him in facedown and released the blade. It slid down and once again, an inch above the man's neck, it suddenly stopped. The crowd cheered and called for the German to be released. "He is innocent!" they cried. "The gods have spoken!"

They took the German out and set him free. Finally they turned to the Polish guy. The executioner looked at him for a moment, then said, "Facedown or faceup?"

"What are you, crazy?" said the Polish guy. "I'm not getting into that thing till they *fix* it!"

* * *

Q: What is the definition of eternity?
A: It's the length of time between when *you* come and *she* leaves.

* * *

A man is having problems because he is not particularly well endowed. As a result of this he is not very confident and has great difficulty with women.

So he goes to a doctor and asks him, "Doctor, is there anything you can do to help me find what I'm looking for?"

The doctor replies, "There is really nothing we can do. We *do* have experimental surgery, but—"

The man interrupts, "Experimental surgery? Tell me about it."

"Well," says the doctor, "we have experimented, but it's not even *tested*—"

"What is it?"

"Well, what we're doing," says the doctor, "is we're experimenting with taking off part of a baby elephant's trunk to give a man the length that he needs, but it's *strictly* experimental——"

"I want the surgery," says the man.

"All right," says the doctor.

So the guy goes in for the surgery, and it works. Two months later he's a changed man. He's got a huge lump in his pants and he feels fabulous.

He goes out on a date with a new young lady, and while they're having dinner together, talking and enjoying the romantic mood, from under the table on his side comes a trunk. It comes out, grabs a hard roll, and goes back under the table.

The girl starts laughing and says, "This is fantastic! Can you do that again?"

The guy says, "I could do it again, but I don't know if my asshole could stand another hard roll!"

*   *   *

Q: Why did the rooster cross the gymnasium?
A: He heard someone say the referee was blowing fouls on the other side.

*   *   *

The brother of a famous Hollywood producer got in my cab one night. We began talking about the work he was doing on his brother's latest film. I asked him if he'd heard any good jokes, and he said, "Yes. This one is very L.A."

A Hollywood producer calls his friend, another Hollywood producer, on the telephone.

"Hello?" his friend answers.

"Hi!" says the man. "This is Robert. How are you doing?"

"Oh," says the friend, "I'm doing great! I just sold a screenplay for two hundred thousand dollars. I just wrote a novel and got a fifty-thousand-dollar advance from the publisher. I also have a television series coming on next week, and everyone says it's going to be a big hit. I'm doing *great*. How are you?"

"Okay," says the first producer. "I'll call you back when you're alone."

* * *

Two men are hunting in the jungle when suddenly they are captured by cannibals. They are taken back to the tribal village and are tied to a tree. The cannibal chief says to the first man, "You've got two choices: death or oogie."

The hunter answers, "Well, I don't want to die, so you'd better give me oogie."

So they take him down to the square in the middle of the village and take all his clothes off him. Then all the male natives take their turns butt-fucking this guy. When all four hundred natives are finished, they drag him back through the town and tie him up to the tree again.

The chief goes up to the second hunter and says, "Okay, you've got two choices: death or oogie."

This guy who has just been watching what happened to his friend says, "Oh, no. You'd better give me death. Just get it over with."

"Okay," says the chief. "But first . . . OOGIE!"

* * *

Two bees are flying along. One looks over at the other and notices that he is wearing a yarmulke. "Hey," the first one says, "why are you wearing that?"

"Oh," says the second one, "I don't want anyone to think that I'm a wasp!"

*　　*　　*

There is a young wrestler who beats everyone in high school, then college, so he decides to enter the Olympics. He does quite well, beating everyone, until there is only one match left and only one wrestler to beat: the Russian. Well, naturally, there is a big national hoopla about it. The Russian against the American for the world championship! There is much publicity and excitement about the contest, and everyone eagerly awaits the big match. The day before it is to occur, the American's coach takes him aside. "Okay, look," says the coach, "you and this Russian are pretty evenly matched. But I have to warn you about one thing. This guy has beaten the last twenty people he's wrestled, and he's beaten them *all* with a move he's got called the Pretzel Hold. Once he gets you into this Pretzel Hold, forget it; there's no way out. So *be careful*. Keep mentally on top of it the *whole* match, and you can beat him. But remember: *Watch out for the Pretzel Hold*!"

"Okay," says the wrestler. "Thanks. I'll be sure to keep on my toes."

The day of the big match comes, and the stands are full. All his friends and family are there, and all the lights, TV cameras, reporters, and eyes of the nation are on this contest.

The American and the Russian both get out on the mat and square off. They circle around each other a few times and then grab each other. They fall to the mat, locked in combat. It turns out to be a very exciting match. First it looks like the Russian will win, then the American. It keeps going back and forth like this for quite a while.

All of a sudden the American loses his concentration for just an instant, and WHAM! The Russian gets him into the Pretzel Hold. And he's got him; he has him pinned. The referee gets down on the mat and slaps the mat once! Twice! And *just* as he's about to slap the mat the third time, the Russian guy goes flying up in the air. He goes up so fast and comes down so hard that he is stunned for a moment. The American jumps on him, pins him, and wins the match.

The crowd goes crazy, everyone screaming and cheering. The stands erupt, and everyone swarms out onto the floor, surrounding the American. All the reporters are gathered around, and they say to the wrestler, "That was incredible! Fantastic! *No one* has ever gotten out of the Pretzel Hold before! How did you *do* it?"

"Well," says the wrestler, "I lost my concentration for just an instant, and that guy got me into the Pretzel Hold so fast, it made my head spin. I heard the referee slap the mat once, twice—and *just* as he was about to slap it the third time, I looked up and saw this testicle hanging there. So I *bit* it. And let me tell you, when you bite your own testicle, you'd be *surprised* what you can do!''

* * *

A jazz musician told me this joke:

Q: What is a VI-IX inversion?
A: It's where the root of the bass is in the mouth of the soprano.

He also told me the famous quote:

"Music is a splendid art but a sad profession."

As I drove my cab down the street I had a feeling I knew what he meant.

* * *

A beautiful, voluptuous woman goes to a gynecologist. The doctor takes one look at this woman and all his professionalism immediately goes out the window. Right away he tells her to undress. After she has disrobed he begins to stroke her thigh. As he does this he says to the woman, "Do you know what I'm doing?"

"Yes," she says, "you're checking for any abrasions or dermatological abnormalities."

"That is correct," says the doctor. He then begins to fondle her breasts. "Do you know what I'm doing now?" he says.

"Yes," says the woman, "you're checking for any lumps or breast cancer."

"That's right," replies the doctor. He then begins

to have sexual intercourse with the woman. He says to her, "Do you know what I'm doing now?"

"Yes," she says. "You're getting herpes."

* * *

Q: Do you know how I make mine twelve inches long?
A: I fold it in half.

* * *

A young nun goes into a liquor store and asks the clerk for a bottle of whiskey.

"I'm afraid, Sister," says the clerk, "that the Mother Superior has left us strict instructions not to sell any liquor to any of you young ladies."

"Oh, but this is *for* the Mother Superior, for medicinal purposes," says the young nun. "You see," she says bashfully, "the Mother Superior is constipated."

"Oh! Excuse me," says the clerk. "In that case, please have this bottle of our finest whiskey. Take it with our compliments and wishes of fine health to the Mother Superior."

"Thank you," says the nun, and she leaves.

A couple of hours later, after he has closed up the store, the clerk is walking down the street when he sees the young nun, swinging on a lamppost and waving the nearly empty whiskey bottle.

"Sister," says the man, walking up to the nun, "I thought you said this whiskey was to go to the Mother Superior for medicinal purposes."

"It is," slurs the nun. "When she sees me, she's gonna *shit*!"

* * *

A gay guy develops a crush on his proctologist, so he makes an appointment with him. As the doctor begins the examination he tells the patient to bend over. The man does this, and the doctor takes one look inside and says, "I can't believe it! There's a bouquet of roses up your ass."

The man then says excitedly, "Read the card! Read the card!"

* * *

Two Polish men are driving along, and they have to stop at a shopping mall. So they find a parking space, get out of the car, slam the doors, and the driver says, "Oh, shit! I just locked the keys in the car!"

"What are we going to do?" says the other man.

"I don't know," replies the driver. "I guess we'll have to break the windshield and get them out."

"No!" says his friend. "You can't break the windshield. Maybe you can find a coat hanger and open the door that way."

"That's too difficult," says the driver.

"Well," says his friend, "you'd better think of something fast because it's starting to rain and the top is down."

* * *

Q: Name which one of these doesn't fit in with the others: AIDS, Herpes, Gonorrhea, and Condominiums.
A: Gonorrhea. You can get rid of gonorrhea.

* * *

A lady is sitting on the bus with her baby when a drunk staggers over in front of the woman, looks down, and says, "Lady, that is the ugliest baby I've ever seen."

The woman starts crying, and everyone on the bus kicks the drunk off. They are making such a big fuss that the bus driver pulls over and stops. He goes to the back of the bus and asks, "What's the matter?"

The woman is inconsolable and can't even talk. She just keeps crying.

"Look, I don't know what he said to you," says the driver, "but to help calm you down I'm going to go get you a cup of tea." He gets off the bus, goes into a delicatessen, and comes back with the tea.

"Calm down," says the driver. "Everything's okay now. See? I brought you this cup of tea and I also brought you a banana for your pet monkey."

*   *   *

Q: What does an accountant do when he is constipated?
A: Works it out with a pencil.

*   *   *

A Polish scientist decides to conduct some experiments with a frog. First he puts the frog on a long table, then says loudly, "Jump, frog, jump!" He records the distance, then cuts off one of the frog's legs. "Jump, frog, jump," he says again, and after the frog manages to jump, he writes down the distance.

It goes on like this with the scientist cutting off a leg at a time, saying, "Jump, frog, jump!" and then recording the distance of the jump. Finally he cuts off the frog's last leg, and says, "Jump, frog, jump." The frog doesn't move. "Jump, frog, jump!" he repeats, and once again, the frog doesn't move.

The scientist then writes out a summary of his experience:

"With four legs frog jumps three feet."
"With three legs frog jumps two feet."
"With two legs frog jumps ten inches."
"With one leg frog jumps three inches."
"With no legs frog loses hearing."

*   *   *

A gorilla goes into a bar and orders a martini. This totally amazes the bartender, but he thinks "What the heck, I guess I might as well make the drink." So he mixes the martini. He then walks back over to give it to the gorilla, and the animal is holding out a ten-dollar bill. Well, now the bartender is just flabbergasted. He can't believe that a gorilla walked into his bar, ordered a martini, and then actuallly had a ten-dollar bill to pay for it.

So, in amazement, he takes the ten and walks to the cash register to make the change. While he's standing in front of the cash register he stops for a second and thinks to himself, "Let me try someting here and see if the gorilla notices anything."

So he walks back over to the gorilla and hands him a dollar change. The gorilla doesn't say anything, he just sits there sipping the martini. After a few minutes the bartender just can't take it anymore.

"You know," he says to the gorilla, "we don't get too many *gorillas* in here."

And the gorilla says, "At nine dollars a drink I'm not surprised."

* * *

A man and woman are about to make love for the first time. As the man takes off his pants the woman looks down and sees that he has five penises.

"That is amazing," she says.

"Yeah," says the man. "I've had them all my life."

"Tell me," says the woman, "how do you wear underwear?"

"It fits," says the man, "like a glove."

* * *

A pretty blond woman is driving along the countryside in her new sports car when something goes wrong with the car and it breaks down. Luckily she happens to be near a farmhouse.

She goes up to the farmhouse and knocks on the door. When the farmer answers, she says to him, "Oh, it's Sunday night and my car broke down! I don't know what I'm going to do! Can I stay here for the night until tomorrow when I can get some help?"

"Well," drawls the farmer, "you can stay here, but I don't want you messin' with my sons Jed and Luke."

She looks through the screen door and sees two young men standing behind the farmer. She judges them to be in their early twenties.

"Okay," she says.

After they have gone to bed for the night the woman begins to get horny just thinking about the two boys in the room next to her. So she quietly goes into their room and says, "Boys, how would you like for me to teach you the ways of the world?"

They say, "Huh?"

She says, "The only thing is, I don't want to get pregnant, so you have to wear these rubbers." She puts them on the boys, and the three of them go at it all night long.

Forty years later Jed and Luke are sitting on the front porch, rocking back and forth.

Jed says, "Luke?"

Luke says, "Yeah, Jed?"

Jed says, "You remember that blond woman that came by here about forty years ago and showed us the ways of the world?"

"Yeah," says Luke, "I remember."

"Well, do you care if she gets pregnant?" asks Jed.

"Nope," says Luke.

"Me, neither," says Jed. "Let's take these things off."

*   *   *

One night I stopped at a diner to have dinner. In the men's room, this was scrawled on the wall:

Dyslexics of the world—Untie!

*　　*　　*

Little Johnny has always wanted to be a carpenter. He is only seven years old, but all he ever talks or thinks about is working with wood. Much to Johnny's delight, a house starts going up right across the street. He asks his mother if he can go out and watch the carpenters work.

She says, "Yes, you may, Johnny. Maybe you will learn something."

So little Johnny goes over and sits on a stump all day long and watches the men at work. After they leave for the day Johnny goes home. His mother greets him and asks "Well, Johnny, did you learn anything today?"

"Yeah," says little Johnny, "a lot!"

"Tell me about it," she says, "What did you learn?"

"Well, first you put up the goddamn door. Then the motherfucker don't fit. So you take it down and shave a cunt hair off each side. Then you put the cocksucker back up."

Johnny's mother is in shock. "Johnny! That's terrible! Just wait till your father gets home!" she says angrily.

A couple of hours later the father comes home, and little Johnny tells him the same story. The father gets really upset and says, "Johnny! Go out back and get me a switch!"

Little Johnny replies, "Fuck you, that's the electrician's job."

*　　*　　*

Two men are sitting at a bar at the top of the World Trade Center. One of the men notices that the other man looks extremely drunk. Suddenly the drunk leans over and says to the man, in words so slurred he can hardly be understood, "I'll bet you...ulp...a hunnert dollars that I can jump out that window there and then jump back in."

The man says to the drunk, "Okay, you've got a bet."

So they each give the bartender a hundred dollars, and while the bartender holds the money, the drunk walks over to the window and jumps out. All is silent for a moment and then all of a sudden, with a loud *swoosh*, the drunk comes back in through the window, landing on his feet. He staggers over to the bar and collects his money.

He then says to the man, "I'll betcha another hunnert dollars I can do it again."

The man is still in shock that the drunk was able to do it in the first place. "He must have just been lucky," he thinks to himself. "A gust of wind must have come along at just the right moment and blown him back in the window. But he couldn't possibly do it *twice*."

So the man says, "All right, I'll bet."

Once again the bartender holds the bet while the drunk weaves over to the window and jumps out.

All is silent, then suddenly, with a loud *swoosh*, the drunk comes back in. Again he stumbles back over to the bar, gets his money, then sits down.

"All right, buddy," says the man, his temper getting the best of him. "If you can do it, *I* can do it! I'll bet you three hundred dollars that I can jump out that window and come right back in."

"All right," slurs the drunk, "you're on."

One more time the bartender holds the bet. The man runs over to the window, jumps out, and plummets straight down to the pavement below, landing with a loud *splat*!

The bartender leans over to the drunk and says, "You know, Superman, sometimes when you drink you really piss me off."

*   *   *

It is not only New Yorkers who have a jaded outlook. I had a man in my taxi once who told me he was from Orlando, Florida.

"I know where that is," I said to him.

"Yeah," the man replied. *"Right near Dismal World."*

*   *   *

A feed salesman is on his way to a farm. As he's driving along at forty m.p.h., he looks out his car window and sees a three-legged chicken running alongside him, keeping pace with his car. He is amazed that a chicken is running at forty m.p.h. So he speeds up to forty-five m.p.h., and the chicken keeps rights up with him with no problem at all.

The man just can't believe this is happening, so he speeds up to sixty, and looks out the window. There is the chicken, not even breathing hard. Then suddenly the chicken just takes off and shoots into the distance.

The man pulls into the farmyard and says to the farmer, "You know, the strangest thing just happened to me. I was driving along at sixty miles an hour, and this three-legged chicken passed me like I was standing still! Do you know anything about it?"

The farmer says, "Yes, that three-legged chicken is our chicken. We raised that chicken."

"Well," says the salesman, "Why did you raise a three-legged chicken?"

"You see, there's me, there's Ma, and there's young Billy, and when we would have chicken for dinner, we would all want a drumstick. We always had to kill two chickens and there would be a lot left over. So we decided to try to breed three-legged chickens so each of us would get a drumstick."

"How do they taste?" asks the salesman.

"Don't know," says the farmer. "We haven't been able to catch one yet."

*   *   *

An old man is talking to his friends. He says, "I've got my health, everything is fine, my heart is good, my liver is good, and my mind, knock wood... who's there?"

*   *   *

A mailman who has been delivering mail on the same route for twenty-five years is about to retire. A lot of people on his route decide to do something nice for him in honor of his retirement. Some people bake cakes, some people put money in an envelope, and pretty much everyone is doing something for the man on his last day on the job.

He gets to one house, and the woman who lives there comes to the door, absolutely naked. She says, "C'mon in."

He looks around, goes inside, and she says, "C'mon upstairs."

He looks around—there is no one there—so he goes upstairs, and she makes love to him. Afterward he is feeling pretty good, and she says to him, "I have a surprise for you. Come downstairs." He goes downstairs and she says, "I'm going to make you breakfast."

The woman then procedes to scramble up some eggs, cook some bacon, squeeze oranges, and gives the man the best breakfast he's ever had. When he finishes eating, she says to him, "Now turn your plate over."

He turns it over and there, stuck to the bottom of the plate, is a dollar bill.

He then says to the woman, "Look, lady, I don't understand. I've been delivering mail to your house for

249

twenty-five years and you never even said as much as hello to me. Now, today, on my last day before I'm retiring, you take me upstairs and make love to me, you make me breakfast, and you give me a dollar bill. I just don't *get* it. What gives?''

"Well," says the woman, "I told my husband that you were retiring and that today would be your last day on the route. When I said that maybe we ought to do something nice for you, he said, 'Fuck 'im. Give him a dollar.'"

The woman pauses a moment, then smiles. "Breakfast," she says, "was my idea."

* * *

The big animals and the little animals are having a football game. Throughout the entire first half the big animals are beating the little animals with a really strong offensive game.

After halftime, when the little animals come out for the third quarter, they are losing 35–0. They kick off to the big animals to begin the second half of play and with great effort, stop them on the twenty-yard line.

On the first down, the big animals send the hippopotamus around the right end. As soon as he gets to the line of scrimmage—BANG!!—he is stopped cold.

Back in the defensive huddle, the squirrel, captain of the little animals, says, "Wow, that was fantastic! Who stopped the hippo like that?"

"It was me," says the centipede.

"Well, keep up the good work!" says the squirrel.

On the second down, the big animals send the rhinocerous around the left end. Once again, he is hit and stopped at the line of scrimmage.

In the huddle again, the squirrel asks, "Who was it this time who stopped the rhino?"

"It was me again," says the centipede.

On the third down, the big animals send the elephant right up the middle. He doesn't get one yard before he is knocked flat on his back.

Once again in the huddle the squirrel asks the centipede, "Was that *you* again?"

"Yes," replies the little bug.

"Tell me," says the squirrel. "Where were you during the first half?"

The centipede answers, "In the locker room, taping my ankles."

* * *

Q: What do you call a skinny Protestant?
A: A Wisp.

* * *

A husband and wife get ready for bed. After they get in bed the man gets up again, goes into the bathroom, and comes back with a glass of water and two aspirin. He gets into the bed and holds out the water and aspirin to his wife until she says, "What are those for?"

The husband says, "They're for you."

The wife says, "Why? I don't have a headache."

The man turns to her and says, "Gotcha!"

* * *

A bartender puts a horse at the end of his bar and hangs a sign around the horse's neck that reads, MAKE ME LAUGH AND WIN $1,000.

251

Many people come into the bar to try to win the prize. After losing they usually hang around drinking for a while discussing with each other how it could be done.

One day a man comes into the bar, sees the sign, and says to the bartender, "You mind if I give it a try?"

"Of course not," says the bartender, chuckling to himself.

The man walks over to the horse and whispers something in the horse's ear. Suddenly the horse bursts into laughter. He laughs and laughs until tears are rolling down his face.

"Okay, buddy," says the bartender, "you win," and gives the man the thousand dollars. The man then walks out of the bar.

About a month later the same man walks into the bar. He sees the horse still down at the end of the bar and asks, "Say, do you still have that contest going on?"

"Well, we do," says the bartender, "but now it's a little different. *Now* you have to make the horse *cry* to win the thousand bucks."

"Well, I can do it," says the man. "But I just need to take the horse out in the back alley for a minute."

"No, no," says the bartender, "you can't take the horse anywhere."

"It'll just be for a minute," says the man, "and I promise I won't hit the horse or hurt him in any way."

"No, no," says the bartender; however everyone else in the bar is so curious to see if the man can do it that they coerce the bartender into agreeing. "All right, all right," he says, "but he can't inflict any pain on the animal."

"I promise I won't," says the man, and leads the horse out into the alley. A minute later he walks back in, with the horse in tears, sobbing uncontrollably.

The bartender gives the man the thousand dollars and the man is about to leave when the bartender says to him, "Excuse me, sir, but before you go, I am really curious. Nobody could even make the horse *laugh* until you came in and did it. Would you mind telling me how you did that?"

"No, I wouldn't mind," says the man. "I made the horse laugh by whispering into his ear that my cock is bigger than his."

"And how," says the bartender, "did you make him cry?"

The man says, "I took it out and showed him."

*　　*　　*

One night I overheard a couple of young men talking in the backseat of my taxi. One of them was telling the other about a blind date he just had. "Boy, was she ugly," he said. "Forget Bette Davis eyes, this girl had Earl Campbell thighs."

*　　*　　*

A midget woman goes to her gynecologist and says, "Doctor, my crotch hurts."

"When," asks the doctor, "does this pain occur?"

"When it is raining out," says the little woman.

"Well, the next time it hurts," says the doctor, "you come to me and I'll see what I can do."

The very next rainy day, in walks the midget woman. "Doc," she says, "my crotch is hurting now."

253

The doctor has the woman lie on the table and put her feet in the stirrups. He covers her knees with a sheet, gets some surgical scissors, and begins snipping away. After a few minutes he says to her, "That should do it."

The woman stands up and says, "Doctor! The pain is completely gone! How did you do it?"

The doctor tells her, "I just cut two inches off the tops of your galoshes."

* * *

Q: What's the difference between a dead snake lying in the road and a dead lawyer lying in the road?
A: There are skid marks in front of the snake.

* * *

A man and woman are divorced in a rather bitter, angry dispute. A few months later the woman remarries. Shortly thereafter the husband accidentally runs into her in a restaurant while she is lunching with one of her woman friends.

"So," says the ex-husband, going up to his ex-wife, "how is your new husband?"

The ex-wife looks up and says, "Oh, he's doing just fine."

"And how," says the man, "does he like your old, tired, worn-out pussy?"

"Oh," says the woman, "he likes it just fine...once he got past the tired and worn-out part."

* * *

Q: How do you get a tissue to dance?
A: You blow a little boogie into it.

* * *

One night I asked a person in my cab (as I often do) what kind of work she did. She replied, "I am a performer at a live sex show on Forty-second Street." I asked her if she enjoyed doing that for a living, and she said that she did, although sometimes it could get to be a bit tiring doing nine shows a day.

As the conversation went on the woman told me that her parents not only knew what kind of job she had, but they also were quite supportive. As a matter of fact, one night her father even came to see her perform.

Before this particular show the woman had told her partner (the man who would be having sex with her on stage) that her father would be in the audience at this performance. The man was quite surprised and a little uneasy at the prospect of the girl's father watching him do his thing with her on stage. She assured him, however, that there would be no problem whatsoever.

They got out on stage and began their act. At one point, while they were getting it on, the woman pointed out her father to her partner. Upon seeing the paternal figure standing over there in the corner, the partner lost his ability to perform.

So, the woman told me, they faked it for the rest of the show and then retired backstage to their dressing room. The woman was laughing, telling the man that he was supposed to be a professional, when suddenly the door opened and the father came in. He walked immediately up to the partner.

"What's your problem?" said the father. *"Isn't my daughter pretty enough for you?"*

* * *

Two men in Ireland are digging a ditch, which happens to be directly across the street from a brothel. Suddenly they see a Protestant minister walk up to the front door of the house of ill repute, look around, then go inside.

"Ah, will you look at that," says one of the ditchdiggers to the other. "What is our world coming to when men of the cloth are visiting such places? It's bloody shameful!"

A few minutes later a rabbi walks swiftly up to the door of the bordello and quietly slips inside.

"Do you believe what we're seein' here, Paddy?" says the ditchdigger. "Why, it's no wonder the young people of today are so confused, with the example the clergymen are setting for them. It's a disgrace!"

Next a Catholic priest quickly enters the whorehouse.

"Ah, what a pity," says the ditchdigger to his friend, "one of the poor girls must be dyin'."

* * *

Q: How many feminists does it take to change a light bulb?

A: One, and there's nothing funny about it.

* * *

A huge building project is going up, and a man must interview several building contractors to find out which company will be chosen to do the construction.

First he interviews a Polish man. "You've seen the plans," says the interviewer. "How much do you think you can do this project for?"

The Polish contractor replies, "I can do it for two hundred thousand dollars."

"That sounds reasonable. How do you break that figure down?"

"One hundred thousand for materials," says the Pole, "and one hundred thousand for labor."

"All right," says the interviewer. "I'll have to get back to you."

The second man, an Italian, comes in. His estimate is four hundred thousand dollars.

"That's a little high," says the interviewer. "How do you break that down?"

"Two hundred thousand for materials," says the Italian, "and two hundred thousand for labor."

"I'll get back to you," says the man.

Finally, in comes a Jewish contractor. When asked for what price he can do the project, he says, "Six hundred thousand dollars."

"That's awfully high!" says the interviewer. "Could you possibly break that figure down for me?"

"Sure," says the Jewish man. "Two hundred thousand for me, two hundred thousand for you, and two hundred thousand for the Polish man."

*　　*　　*

Not since the fictional James Bond has the world seen the likes of the masterful Irish undercover agent Murphy the Spy. The allied forces use him only once or twice a year and only for missions of extreme importance, missions that might fail if not for the great talents of Murphy the Spy.

Only a few days ago just such a mission arose. But even the intelligence agencies do not know how to contact Murphy the Spy directly. All that is known is that when he is not directly involved in espionage activities, he retires to a small village near the Irish coastline.

Armed only with Murphy's secret password—"The weather looks fine now, but it might rain later"—an agent from the CIA sets out for the small town on the Irish coast. As he arrives in the village the CIA man decides that the most logical place to start his search is the local pub.

After sitting in the pub for a couple of hours the agent is finally alone with the bartender. "Say," he says to him, "do you have anyone in this town by the name of ... Murphy?"

"Oh, sure!" says the bartender. "Right next door we have Murphy the Baker! Why, I bet if you went in there right now, he'd be more than happy to help you in any way he can!"

"I'm not sure," says the CIA man, "that Murphy the Baker is the man I'm looking for. Do you have anyone else named Murphy in this town?"

"Ah, yes, we certainly do!" answers the bartender. "At the church on top of the hill we have Father Murphy. And a kindly old gentleman he is! Now—"

"I don't think he's the one, either," interrupts the man, looking around furtively. "Do you by any chance have another Murphy nearby?"

"Well, of course," says the bartender, "up the road about a mile we have Murphy the Solicitor. If you go there right now, you'll probably find him in."

"No," says the agent, "I don't think that's him, either. Aren't there any *other* Murphys in this town?"

"Certainly there are! There are quite a few!" says the bartender. "As a matter of fact, *my* name happens to be Murphy."

"It is?" says the spy. He moves in closer to the bartender and says, "The weather looks fine now, but it might rain later."

"Oh!" says the bartender, pounding the bar. "You're looking for Murphy the *Spy*!"

* * *

What bird is traditionally associated with warlike tendencies and aggression?

The hawk.

What bird is associated with peace and love?

The dove.

What bird is traditionally associated with childbirth and the delivery of children?

The stork.

What bird is associated with birth control?

The swallow.

* * *

Dirty Ernie is in class one day when the teacher announces that their homework assignment that night will be to find out how to use the word *beautiful* in a sentence. The next day, when they come into school, the teacher says, "Okay, Alice, stand up and use the word *beautiful* in a sentence."

"Well, yesterday," begins Alice, "when I walked home, I saw a beautiful patch of flowers."

"Very good," says the teacher. "Now, Susie?"

Susie stands up and says, "Well, last night after school my mother took me to the store and bought me a beautiful dress."

"Very good, Susie," says the teacher. "Ernie?"

Ernie puts his cigarette and beer under the desk and stands up. "Well, last night," he says, "I was sitting there watching television when my sister comes home. She says, 'Hey, Dad, I'm pregnant,' and my old man says, 'Beautiful, just beautiful.'"

* * *

Q: In the Jewish faith when does the fetus become a human being?

A: When it graduates from medical school.

*   *   *

An undertaker escorts a grieving widow in to see the masterful work he has just finished on her dear, recently departed husband. She takes one look and cries, "Oh, no! What have you done? It's all wrong!"

"What, madam," asks the bewildered mortician, "could possibly be wrong?"

"Where," says the woman, sobbing, "is the brown suit I bought for him? I got it especially for this occasion!"

The man looks down and see that indeed the woman's husband is wearing a navy blue suit. He then glances at the cadaver in the next room and immediately realizes his error. The other corpse is wearing the brown suit.

"I'm terribly sorry, madam," says the undertaker, "but I think I can correct this problem momentarily." He says to his assistant, who is standing nearby and has seen what has happened, "John, please take Mrs. Smith into my office for a moment."

As the assistant takes Mrs. Smith's hand and leads her into the office, the mortician quickly wheels the husband's body into the adjoining room, next to the other corpse. Three minutes later he goes into the office and gets the widow.

Leading the woman back into the main room, he says to her, "I think you'll find this much more to your liking."

The woman looks down and sees her husband in

the brown suit. She sighs deeply and says, "Yes, that's perfect. That's how I always want to remember him."

After she leaves the assistant turns to the undertaker and says, "Wow! That was fantastic! How did you manage to change those suits so quickly?"

"I didn't," says the undertaker. "I just switched heads."

*   *   *

A father and son are walking down the street when they happen to walk by two dogs mating. When asked by the boy what they are doing, the father replies, "Son, they are making puppies."

That night the little boy wakes up because he is thirsty. He goes to his parents' bedroom, opens the door, and discovers them in the act of making love.

"What are you doing?" he asks.

"Son, we're making babies," the father replies.

"Oh," says the boy. "Well, could you turn Mommy over? I think I'd rather have a puppy."

*   *   *

Q: How does a macho man know when a woman has had an orgasm?
A: A macho man doesn't care.

*   *   *

It's six o'clock in the morning. The toe looks over at the penis and says, "Psst! Hey!"

The penis stands up. "Yeah?" he says.

"You know, man," says the toe to the penis, "I've

262

really got it tough. Every morning this guy gets up, shoves me into a stinking old sock, ties me up in this dirty old shoe, walks on me all over town, and people step on me all day long."

The penis just looks at the toe and says, "Fella, you ain't got no problems at all. This guy gets up every day and shoves *me* into a size thirty jockstrap, and it's too tight. So I choke all day long. Then he goes over to his girlfriend's house, starts messing around with her, and I get all tense and excited, and I can't move a muscle. Then he shoves this rubber balloon over my head, locks me in a big hairy cage, and makes me do push-ups until I get sick and throw up."

* * *

Q: What do you get when you cross an onion and a donkey?
A: A piece of ass that brings tears to your eyes.

* * *

After dropping some people off at Tavern on the Green during the height of the Christmas season, I was about to pull out onto Central Park West when a man and woman approached my cab. The woman tapped on my window, so I rolled it down.

"Do you know," she asked, "where I can find the exposition with the three wise guys?"

I managed to choke back my laughter long enough to tell them that I didn't know where it was, and I was able to drive off before giving in to the temptation of saying to her, "You mean Moe, Larry, and Curly?"

* * *

A thief walks into a store.

He waits until he is alone in the store with the manager, then pulls out a gun. "Okay," he says, pointing the pistol at the trembling man, "go over to the cash register and give me all the money."

"All right," says the man, "all right. I'll do anything you say. Just please don't hurt me."

After the manager has emptied the cash register the crook says, "Okay, pull your pants down and bend over."

"Oh, no," says the man, "not that."

"Just do it," says the robber. The manager drops his trousers, and the crook proceeds to have his way with him.

When the robber is finished, he tells the man to turn around.

The thief says, "Okay, just one more thing before I leave. Give me a blow job."

"No! No!" says the manager. "Please, not that! Oh please, no!"

The crook puts the gun to the man's temple and says, "Do it."

So the guys gets down on his knees and begins giving the robber a blow job. After a few minutes the thief starts getting carried away and starts moaning and waving his hands around in the air above his head.

The manager suddenly stops and says to the crook, "Say, could you please put that gun back up to my head in case one of my friends walks in?"

*   *   *

There are two jazz musicians who are great buddies. They hang out together and play together for years. They are virtually inseparable. Unfortunately one of them gets hit by a truck and killed. About a week later his friend wakes up in the middle of the night with a start because he can feel a presence in the room. He calls out, "Who's there? Who's there? What's going on?"

He hears a faraway voice say, "It's me—Bob."

Excitedly he sits up in bed.

"Bob! Bob! Is that you? Where are you?"

"Well," says the faraway voice, "I live in heaven now."

"You do? You live in *heaven*! Oh, my gosh! What's it like?"

"Well," says Bob, "I gotta tell you, I'm jamming up here every day. I'm playing with Bird and 'Trane, and Count Basie just got in a little while ago! Man, it is *smoking*!''

"Oh, wow!" says his friend. "That sounds fantastic! Tell me more, tell me more!"

"Let me put it this way," says the voice. "There's good news and there's bad news. The *good* news is that these guys are in *top form*. I mean, I have *never* heard them sounding better. They are *wailing* up here.

"The *bad* news is that God has this girlfriend who sings. . . . ''

* * *

A young boy needs to go to the bathroom, but he'll only do it with his grandmother. He can't go by himself. So he says to his father, "Daddy, I have to go pee. Can you go get Grandma?"

The father says, "That's all right. Don't bother your Grandma. I'll take you to the bathroom."

"No, no," says the boy. "I want my grandmother."

"Why," says the father, "must you always go to the bathroom with your grandmother?"

The boy replies, "Because her hand shakes."

Years later the grandmother goes to the doctor and says, "Doctor, I'm losing my sex urge."

The doctor says, "Madam, you're ninety-three years old. You should be glad you even have a sex urge."

"I understand," says the woman, "but I still want more of a sex drive."

"All right," he says, "when did you first start noticing this?"

"She says, "Last night and then again this morning."

The doctor says, "Your problem isn't that you're losing your sex urge, your problem is that you're not having enough sex. You should be having sex fifteen times a month."

So she goes home to her husband and says, "Pop, guess what? The doctor says I should be having sex fifteen times a month."

The husband then says, "Great! Put me down for five."

She dies a few months later, but they save the baby. At the funeral her husband is very upset. His friend comes over to comfort him. The old man says, "She was a wonderful girl. But, above all, she was a fabulous lover, and I'll never find another like her."

His friend says, "Listen, you're a strong, vital man. You're gonna find another woman and start all over again."

"I know," says the old man, "but what am I gonna do *tonight*?"

His friend says, "Why don't you go to a house of ill repute?"

So, the old man goes to one, knocks on the door, and the madam answers. "Can I help you?" she says.

The man says, "Yes. I'd like a woman for the night."

The madam says, "How *old* are you?"

He says, "I am ninety-six years old."

She says, "Ninety-six years old? You've *had* it."

"I have?" says the old man. "How much do I owe you?"

Anyway, he walks inside and says, "So, tell me something. How much is this going to cost me?"

The madam says, "Well, you're ninety-six years old; that'll be ninety-six dollars."

The man says, "You're putting me on!"

She says, "That'll be another ten dollars."

So he goes upstairs with a nice young lady, and he says to her, "Tell me, do you know how to do it the Jewish way?"

She says, "No."

He says, "Well, then, forget it."

"Wait a minute," the girl says. "I'm new at this game and I'm eager to please. You show me how to do it the Jewish way and I'll give it to you for half price."

He says, "That's *it*!"

Two weeks later he develops a urinary problem, so he goes to the doctor. He says, "Doc, I can't urinate."

The doctor says, "You're ninety-six years old. You've urinated enough."

"But, wait," says the old man, "Look, I have a discharge."

So the doctor examines the man's penis. He then asks. "When did you last have sex?"

"A week ago," says the man.

"Well, that's what it is," says the doctor. "You're coming."

The doctor then says, "How are your bowel movements?"

The man says, "I move my bowels every morning at eight o'clock."

"That's great," says the doctor.

"No, it's not," says the old man. "I don't get out of bed until ten."

As a result of this, he goes into an old-age home. After two weeks of consistantly defecating in his bed, the nurse says to him, "You do that one more time and you're cleaning it up yourself."

The next morning he does it again. The nurse walks in, takes one look, and says, "That's it! *You* clean it up!" and walks out the door.

So the man picks the sheets up off his bed and disgustedly throws them out the window. They happen to land on a drunk walking on the street below.

The drunk wildly wrestles the sheets off his head, runs into the nearest bar, and says, "Give me a double martini—quick!"

The bartender says, "Hey, buddy, what happened to you?"

"You're not going to believe this," says the drunk, "but I just beat the *crap* out of a ghost!"

* * *

One night (*actually it was about six in the morning, but I never count it as the next day until I've gone to sleep*) *as I was returning home after driving my usual twelve-hour shift, I asked the cabbie driving me home if he'd heard any good jokes. He said, "Yeah, and this is the only cab driver joke you'll ever hear." Well, since then I have heard a few others, but I still like this one the best:*

A cab driver is driving along when a man hails him, so he pulls over and the man gets in. In a very proper English accent the man says, "London, England, please."

The cab driver turns around to the man and says, "You know, out-of-town is double the meter. London is about two thousand dollars *on* the meter. So we're talking about a four-thousand-dollar fare here."

"That's all right," says the gentlemen. "I'll give you a good tip as well."

So they drive out to Kennedy Airport and get onto a cargo plane. They fly over to England and get out at Heathrow Airport. They drive into London, and the cab driver drops the man off in Kensington. True to his word, the man gives the cabbie the fare and an eight-hundred-dollar tip.

So the cab driver feels great. He says to himself, "Wow, this is *great*. I've never *had* such a good day. And, gee, I've never been to England before, either. I might as well drive around a little bit and check it out. Who knows, maybe I'll even pick up a fare or two."

Sure enough, after about half an hour a little man in a bowler hat carrying an umbrella hails him. The cab driver pulls over, and the man gets in.

In an accent as proper as the other Englishman's, the gentleman says, "Flatbush Avenue, please, New York City."

The cab driver turns around angrily and says, "*I don't go to Brooklyn!*"

If you ever do get into my cab, though, I want you to know that I do go to Brooklyn—or anywhere else you want to go. Hope to see you sometime!